School Budget Mastery

Julie Cordiner & Nikola Flint

Updated October 2020
First published in Great Britain in 2018
by School Financial Success Publications

ISBN: 0995590206
ISBN-13: 978-0995590205

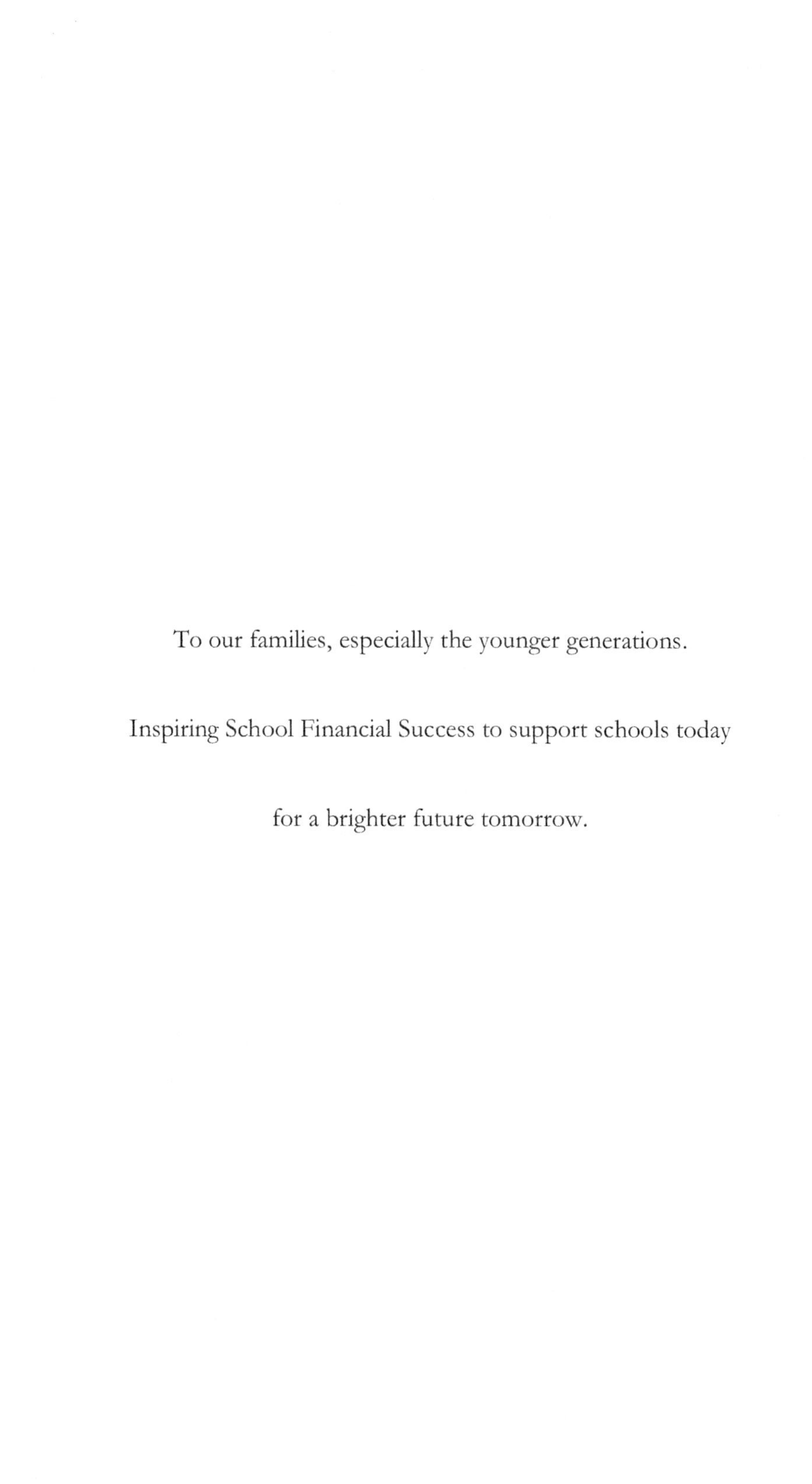

To our families, especially the younger generations.

Inspiring School Financial Success to support schools today

for a brighter future tomorrow.

CONTENTS

FOREWORD

These are challenging times for leaders in education, when they need to be able to handle a wide range of issues if their schools are to thrive and provide the best possible outcomes for the children and young people in their care. One of the biggest challenges that many leaders are facing is how to keep their school afloat financially.

We've been through a difficult period recently, when funding has not increased in line with rising cost pressures. There have been delays in the expected school funding reforms, and only after a sustained period of lobbying did the government agree to provide more money. Meanwhile, across the country reserves are shrinking, some schools have fallen into deficit and others have seen existing deficits increase.

The situation needs skilful financial leadership. Yet how well prepared are school leaders and governors for the work that needs to be done to achieve sustainable budgets, within the context of today's high stakes accountability and other pressures such as changes in the needs of pupils? Do aspiring headteachers and principals have sufficient training and practical experience in financial leadership to prepare them for taking charge of a (multi-)million-pound budget when they are first appointed?

Do even experienced heads and School Business Leaders have the right tools when moving to a new school and being faced with an inherited financial problem on a different scale to what they have known before, among all the usual challenges? Are governors able to identify when action is not being taken early enough to avoid a potential deficit and do they have the knowledge and skills to steer the school through a recovery plan?

This book takes the subject of school budgeting and works through it in a systematic way, teaching not only the basics, but going further to support a detailed understanding of cultural, behavioural and technical issues. The principles apply equally to schools and academies. Whatever your role, you will find it helpful in seeing the bigger picture and supporting your school to achieve a meaningful set of financial plans.

1 INTRODUCTION

Challenging Times

School funding is a complex topic at the best of times, but in the current climate it presents particular challenges for school leaders. Many schools are dealing with increases in pupil numbers and a rising complexity of needs in children and young people. There is the same relentless pressure to keep on improving standards, amid frequent changes in accountability measures.

Yet funding has not kept pace with the need to spend, especially in relation to increasing employment costs. The need to respond to the Covid-19 pandemic has placed further strain on the whole education sector. These tensions in the system are causing severe problems for schools, and it's particularly difficult for those that have historically been underfunded.

Another issue has been the ongoing uncertainty in how much money schools will have in the future, as a result of delays in school funding reform. The National Funding Formula (NFF) was at last introduced in 2018/19, changing the pattern of Dedicated Schools Grant (DSG) allocations in an attempt to address the 'postcode lottery' of funding. The proposals went through a number of changes, as the government realised the political difficulties in trying to redistribute funds in a time of austerity. The ultimate plan for schools to be directly funded by DfE has also suffered delays, and will not now be introduced before 2022/23.

Schools are constantly searching for the best strategies to achieve improvements in outcomes for learners. Some come at a high cost but have low effectiveness, others are cheaper and highly effective, and there are all shades in between. At a time when there are lots of competing pressures for available resources, school leaders need to be more careful than ever in how they decide to spend their money.

The key to achieving improvement within a restricted budget is making sure you are delivering value for money. This needs to be a deliberate strategy rather than something that is left to chance. The importance of being in control of your finances has never been greater, but the barriers to achieving this are also mounting.

So, how can you handle these challenges? We believe the best approach is to make plans for how you are going to use your resources wisely, putting the school budget at the heart of your vision.

At a time of uncertainty, it can be difficult to make plans, especially for a period longer than a year; the best you can say is that they will inevitably have to change. But it is better to exercise some measure of control by developing a strategy, than to allow your educational boat to be tossed about by the storms.

A strategic plan, involving a clear financial vision expressed through your budget, will help you to work towards the school's aims in an organised, coherent and confident way. You might think this is not possible with so many changes in the wind, but don't let that put you off.

There are two important things you can do to help make any sort of planning less daunting: state the assumptions on which your plan is based, and be prepared to be flexible in how you implement it. The high-level vision won't change, but some of the approaches and actions might need to be flexed to suit changing circumstances and the level of resources at your disposal. This is equally true of financial planning.

Simply having a plan will help you to feel more in control, because you will be sketching out a course with a journey and an end point in mind that are of your own choosing. It helps others, particularly staff and governors, to understand what the school is trying to achieve and consider how they can play their part in achieving it.

As the famous saying goes (variously attributed to Benjamin Franklin or Alan Lakein), 'If you fail to plan, you are planning to fail'.

School budgeting as a planning tool

Robust planning is essential for an effective school budget. You need to work out how much you can afford to spend, and what it should best be spent on. If those responsible for taking decisions on expenditure don't understand the priorities that you want to focus your spending on, or if they don't know what good value for money looks like, you may find your money disappearing faster than the food on your pupils' plates at lunchtime.

We're not pretending that school budgeting is easy in the current climate. For one thing, we are no nearer multi-year allocations of funding, which is a crucial element of the information that's needed to help schools build budget forecasts for the medium term. Prior to the introduction of the NFF, the per pupil grant (Dedicated Schools Grant - DSG) paid to individual local authorities for school budgets was fairly predictable, rolled forward each year with only minor tweaks. Funding may not have kept pace with costs, but at least schools generally didn't have to cope with volatility in their allocations, unless they were related to pupil numbers and characteristics.

Before the reforms, schools were therefore able to estimate future funding for a three to five-year period with a reasonable degree of certainty, as the starting point for their multi-year budget planning. Since 2018/19, that level of stability has not been guaranteed, and under the initial phase of the NFF, funding has been dependent on individual local authorities (LAs) deciding how far they should try to reflect the NFF values in their local funding formulae. Unfortunately, due to the government's Spending Review cycle, there is always a cliff edge for future indications of DSG allocations and school funding arrangements. We will go into this in more detail later.

'School Budget Mastery' in context

The next few years will be very difficult for many schools, as they continue to grapple with changing pupil numbers and needs, continuing pressure to achieve improved outcomes, and levels of funding that may or may not be sufficient to cover rising costs. This book provides advice and support to help school leaders, senior managers and governors be more confident in their ability to achieve a sustainable budget.

Our guidance will help you to develop a comprehensive understanding of school budgeting, whether you are a new or existing headteacher, School Business Leader, middle leader, or the Chair of the Governing Board, Board of Trustees or Finance Committee. Alternatively, you may be performing another role, and simply want an insight into how the whole process works.

This book will also be of particular interest to middle and senior leaders who aspire to headship, as a way of preparing for the financial responsibilities that go with the role. This is a topic that isn't always easy to grasp in theoretical modules within professional qualifications, and it can be daunting to be put in charge of a school budget for the first time. During your career so far, you have focused your attention on aspects of teaching and learning, and now you are expected to juggle finances as well. Even though a headteacher may have an excellent School Business Leader to rely on, legally the responsibility delegated by the governors lies firmly with the most senior leader. By reading our guide, you will give yourself a head start and be more confident when that time comes.

The book doesn't only guide you through the steps involved in the actual preparation and monitoring of a school budget; it also takes a broader approach to ensure that this subject is placed in context. We therefore discuss issues such as creating a culture of financial leadership and the leading roles of headteachers and governors. Because the funding changes may trigger some challenges and opportunities, depending on their impact on your school, we take time to explain what the reforms mean.

Throughout the book, we reinforce the importance of a value for money approach, whether you need to make savings or not. Assessing the contribution that spending makes to the achievement of your aims will help you to make sure that your budget is targeted to the activities that make the biggest difference to outcomes for pupils. This may allow you to release savings by stopping expenditure that doesn't have a positive impact, or if you're lucky, it could help you to achieve more success with any extra funding that you might receive under the NFF arrangements. Every little helps.

While the main focus is on the annual budget, we also provide tips on strategic financial planning for the medium term, so that you can start to think about making your financial approach sustainable.

'School Budget Mastery' is part of a series of guidebooks designed to help school leaders make the best use of the resources they are given to achieve sustainable budgets in challenging times. Two others are particularly relevant to this topic:

- **Leading a School Budget Review**

  A step-by-step process for leading a detailed review of the school budget.

- **Forecasting Mainstream School Funding** (new in November 2020)

  A practical toolkit to help you prepare high-level multi-year funding projections based on best, middle and worst-case funding scenarios for all aspects of funding. It also contains guidance on developing a Financial Sustainability Plan.

At the end of this book you will find a link to the Books page on our website, so you can find information on all our publications as they appear.

To be fully informed about developments in school funding and find out when we are launching new books and online courses, visit our website at https://schoolfinancialsuccess.com. Here you can read our blog posts and sign up for a free monthly newsletter containing the latest government announcements on finance and funding. This will help you keep up to date, which is an essential part of leadership.

Aims of the book

What benefits are there in reading this book? We aim to provide:

- insights into how to create a culture of financial leadership in a school;
- an explanation of the current school funding system;
- information to enhance your understanding of the roles of governors and the headteacher in relation to finance;
- an overview of budgeting approaches, the budget cycle and available funding sources;
- guidance on how to plan ahead, ensuring all relevant information is available before you start to prepare the budget;
- an outline of the steps to take in preparing your annual school budget and what to do if it doesn't balance;
- details of monitoring processes to ensure the budget is kept under control;
- advice on strategic financial planning.

School budgeting will become even more important in the coming years as a mechanism to ensure that a school's priorities can be delivered within the scarce resources that are available, and that you can cope with any changes that might derail your plans. At stake is the ability of all children and young people to realise their full potential; they deserve the best possible education.

Focusing on the development of an effective budget process is an essential aspect of financial management. Indeed, it is the starting point, so we hope that this book is a timely source of advice and support. Our aim is to help you master the art of preparing a school budget in a way that supports your vision, ensures it can be delivered by the end of the financial year and helps to keep your school in a sustainable financial position.

2 FINANCIAL LEADERSHIP

What is Financial Leadership?

In a climate of uncertainty, schools need to work out what is under their control, and take decisions in the best interests of pupils, while developing a strategy to manage the risks in relation to aspects that they can't control.

We believe that finance is an integral part of school leadership, sufficiently important to be considered in a category of its own: school financial leadership. So let's start by clarifying what financial leadership is and understand why it is essential, especially in the current climate.

At the highest level, strategic financial leadership involves creating a vision for how the available resources will be used to achieve your school's aims in the longer term, and implementing that vision in a way that creates the conditions for sustainable improvement. Curriculum, staffing and school development plans are all linked with the budget, to create an interwoven, mutually compatible set of planning documents. Together, these form a blueprint to drive the school forward.

Leaders also need to model behaviours in relation to finances. This means taking a responsible approach to the use of public money and ensuring proper accountability through compliance with legal requirements. Unfortunately, there are examples of schools and academies carrying out illegal transactions and disregarding conflicts of interest by awarding contracts to people who are connected to leaders, Trustees or governors. This sort of behaviour undermines the whole education system, and causes significant concern among the majority of school leaders who are upright and honest. Published reports provide some salutary lessons about the ease with which financial regulations can be ignored if governors and senior or middle leaders are not watchful enough.

At a more practical level, financial leadership involves translating the vision into reality, coordinating all the different strands of financial decision-making to achieve value for money across the whole school. That means making sure that in spending the school's money, you are eliminating waste, being as efficient as possible and targeting resources to the activities that have the greatest impact on outcomes.

You will already be familiar with the use of self-evaluation and inspection results to identify strengths and areas for improvement. Financial leadership takes this a stage further by making sure that you target resources on the areas that need investment to secure improvement. Any comparisons with similar schools should include a check on what they are spending to achieve their results for a given profile of pupils. If they are spending less and achieving more for a similar profile of pupils, it is worth exploring further.

But financial leadership isn't the sole preserve of the headteacher. They will undoubtedly set the tone, but it needs a team effort across the whole school, with each member of staff playing their part to create a unified approach. If the team is the orchestra playing a piece of music composed by senior leaders and governors, the headteacher is the conductor, prompting the sections when they need to come to the fore, and turning the volume up or down as appropriate to create the right blend. Each individual player creates a sound on a single instrument, but they need to be brought together in perfect time to create the right effect. The culture and practice of financial behaviours in a school should work in the same way.

Financial leadership is crucial in a time of uncertainty. It gives confidence to staff, leaders, governors, parents, and funding bodies that the school has a robust approach and is in control of its finances.

Staff will be looking for reassurance that their employment is not at risk. No school leader can give a cast iron guarantee of how many staff the school will need in the future, but strong financial leadership will give staff confidence that the school's stability is being maintained through forward financial planning and effective use of resources, and that any decisions made are in the best interests of the pupils. Maintaining confidence in the school's viability will help you retain high quality staff.

At a time of so many challenges, everyone will want to know that you are making the most of the resources available to deliver the school's vision. Otherwise you are at risk of having a fine set of plans that can't be achieved.

The budget is the means by which you deliver your vision; if you don't make provision for the cost of initiatives, they are unlikely to happen. You will also be judged on your ability to achieve expenditure and income broadly in line with the plans outlined in your budget. This is an important measure of accountability to governors and to the organisation that provides your funding, whether that is the local authority or the government. We will now consider the overall approach that will best achieve this.

Promoting a greater understanding of budgeting

In the above discussion, we've indicated the importance of the school budget as a practical tool for achieving your plans. It binds together all the school's activities in financial terms, by showing how the money will be spent. The accuracy of the budget is therefore a key accountability measure.

Once you master the skill of reading a budget, you can develop the ability to analyse what is going on in the school relatively quickly. In this book, we will provide pointers to the key messages you can look for when planning and monitoring your budget, to measure the achievement of your vision.

If you are going to set a realistic budget and keep to it, you will need to promote a greater understanding of budget planning and monitoring throughout the school. You might think that the budget is only relevant to senior leaders and those with financial responsibilities. But there is a need for a wider section of the school community to understand it, beyond senior and middle leaders. It is a matter of judging the right level of information to give to different types of staff.

This means that you need to involve governors, classroom teachers, teaching assistants, and administrative and other support staff. The level of involvement will depend on their role, but everyone can make some contribution to the school achieving a sustainable budget. It doesn't only concern members of staff who are responsible for purchasing or using resources; everybody has a part to play. Think of it in the widest sense: staff, premises, equipment and money. Whether they are budget holders or not, all staff are paid from the budget, and therefore the way in which they spend their time can have a big influence on whether value for money is achieved.

Consider how much of your budget is spent on staff. The way you use them is crucial; everyone needs to work at maximum efficiency. Do you, your leadership team and governors know how much it costs per day to run the school, or the average cost per hour of all the teachers across the school? How much does an average lesson cost to deliver, including classroom support staff and all the equipment and resources used?

Making this sort of average cost information widely known among senior colleagues can have quite an impact. Once everyone understands the cost of a staff meeting, it's surprising how ways can be found to run it more efficiently, allowing everyone to spend their time on work that has a more direct impact in the classroom.

It is important to encourage senior leaders to think creatively. They should be advocates for a value for money mindset in other staff, encouraging them to find ways of achieving savings with the lowest possible negative impact on school improvement. They may be able to act as champions for particular areas of expenditure, tasked with making resources go further. Asking them to record savings achieved on an ongoing basis can be a great motivator. In Chapter 16 we suggest ways of building in some finance-related targets into appraisal objectives for different types of staff, including middle leaders.

If every member of staff understands the broad approach being taken to guarantee that the school's finances are being used wisely, they will all be able to work together efficiently and effectively to achieve the school's aims. Everyone will understand the importance of achieving value for money and can share the responsibility for keeping within budget.

Staff should be encouraged to look on the school's budget as if it is their own money. In fact, it is their own money, because the funding the school receives is generated from the taxes they pay!

Succession planning for leadership is another reason to raise awareness of finance, not just for your school, but for the education system as a whole. Many aspiring headteachers don't receive enough financial training before they take up their first headship and inherit what can be a multi-million-pound budget. Even if it is given due emphasis in formal leadership programmes, Deputy and Assistant Headteachers are not always given full practical experience of setting and managing a budget in their own school.

With the prospect of continuing unfunded cost pressures for many schools during the coming years, it is essential that future leaders are equipped with the skills they need to ensure that a school stays afloat financially. Existing headteachers, whether they were in a school leadership role during the last period of significant funding cuts in the early 1990s or not, will also benefit from taking a fresh look at strategies for financial sustainability. A different leadership toolkit is needed to survive the choppy waters we are sailing on.

3 SCHOOL FUNDING REFORM

The funding context for your budget

The starting point for your school budget is the amount of money you receive. Delays in the full introduction of the National Funding Formula (NFF), intended to achieve fairer funding, have created huge uncertainty for schools, making it difficult to plan ahead. It's taken some time for the government to be persuaded of the need to increase funding, although whether it will keep pace with cost pressures is still doubtful.

If you don't have information on which to base your decisions, it's very tempting to put your head in the sand and wait. For some schools, this has proved disastrous. By failing to take action to find savings, they have seen balances rapidly reduce, fallen into deficit, or increased an existing deficit.

Once in deficit, it can be extremely difficult to recover, and there is a risk of budget cuts undermining educational achievement and progress. A school in budget difficulties is not an attractive prospect, and it can affect both recruitment and retention of good staff. If financial problems hit the media, it can affect applications for places, and falling rolls means less funding.

The level of funding you receive therefore provides a very important context for your school budget.

School funding reforms have focused on the distribution of grants to address the historic postcode lottery of wide variations in funding allocations between similar schools in different geographical areas. This was due to the use of historic allocations for grants to LAs and the existence of a local formula in every LA. Over time, the DfE limited LA freedoms, but the starting point for the NFF was still an uneven pattern that was hard to justify.

There are many different aspects to the NFF, but we have divided them into the following areas:

- Progress towards the NFF: a brief history
- The fundamentals of the NFF

- Level of funding and transition to the NFF
- Impact of the High Needs NFF on mainstream school budgets
- Will funding be enough to cover cost pressures?
- How to keep informed.

Progress towards the NFF: a brief history

It is a shame that previous governments didn't grasp the nettle of fairer funding when it was originally mooted over ten years ago, because the economic situation would then have allowed a true levelling-up of resources for schools. As soon as the Coalition Government introduced austerity measures in 2010, it became evident that without extra money being made available, a national formula would inevitably lead to winners and losers. Taking money from one set of schools to give it to others who are regarded as underfunded is never a palatable message for politicians to deliver.

In 2016, it looked as if the reforms would at last become a reality, with two consultations on a National Funding Formula, one on high level principles and approaches, and another explaining the intended distribution.

At that stage, the intention was to introduce the reforms in 2017/18, initially using the national formula to calculate the grants for individual LAs, who would still distribute it to schools according to a local formula. This was dubbed the '**Soft NFF**'. DfE aimed to move to the second stage, the '**Hard NFF**', in 2019/20. This would cut LAs out of the picture, with the government setting allocations for every school in the country.

These proposals involved losses for a significant number of schools, phased over the period up to 2020, causing a very public realisation of the potential impact of the policy.

However, the timetable was disrupted by the political changes that occurred after the vote to leave the EU, and the NFF was delayed to 2018/19. The General Election in 2017 brought school funding into the political arena to a much greater degree. Sustained campaigns by the whole education community achieved some success in persuading the government to put more money into the pot, in order to avoid cash losses for some schools. We discuss this in the section below on funding levels and transition to the NFF.

The final decision in September 2017 confirmed the Soft NFF would be introduced in 2018/19 and remain in place for 2019/20. However, Ministers decided to extend it into 2020/21, as a majority of local authorities had moved towards the NFF values. In July 2020, the DfE announced another extension, allowing local formulae to continue in 2021/22.

Under the Soft NFF, LAs do not have to use the NFF values in the local formula. However, some LAs may find it increasingly difficult to maintain a different approach, firstly because the amount of funding they receive is calculated using the national formula, and secondly because they have to comply with various restrictions to ensure schools are not adversely affected. Most LAs have already adopted the NFF or seem to be working towards it.

Direct funding of all schools by DfE (the Hard NFF) requires primary legislation, so there will be some signs to indicate whether it can be achieved in 2022/23 as the Parliamentary timetable develops during 2021.

It isn't only Brexit and Covid-19 which have contributed to the delay in fully implementing the NFF. There are some difficult technical issues which need to be resolved, mostly involving so-called 'historic spend' items. These are currently allocated at LA level, based on the previous year's budgeted expenditure by the LA. They include rates, funding for split sites, Private Finance Initiative costs and exceptional premises features.

Finding a way of converting these into a formulaic approach is pretty challenging. It is also hard to imagine how funding for SEND can be managed in isolation under the Hard NFF, as the current flexibility to move money between the Schools and High Needs blocks will probably cease.

The Hard NFF could cause a substantial increase in demand on the ESFA's capacity, as the number of mainstream schools they will have to deal with will rise from around 8,700 academies (at August 2020) to a total of over 20,600 including LA primary and secondary schools. Specialist settings will still be funded from the LA's High Needs Budget. Savings in LA budgets will be minimal, as this work is usually carried out by one or two finance and data experts in a couple of months, and it is only part of their role.

The fundamentals of the NFF

The basic principles of school funding have not changed in the new system: funding still follows pupils and additional weightings continue to be given to particular pupil and school characteristics that affect the need to spend. Examples of these are deprivation, low prior attainment, English as an Additional Language and small rural schools.

However, the NFF means that in the long term, when DfE is funding all schools directly, there will be a single national formula with values decided by the government, rather than local decisions by the LA.

The factors within the NFF have remained broadly the same as under the previous system, except for the removal of the Looked After Children factor, where the funding has been transferred into Pupil Premium Plus grant for LAC. A minor factor, the post 16 adjustment, was also removed (not the main post 16 grant, but a historic adjustment used by a few LAs). There have been changes in the weighting given to some factors.

Each year, the DfE publishes a policy document which includes the factors and unit values for primary and secondary schools. For future years, you will be able to find the relevant paper by searching for 'Policy paper National Funding Formula for schools and high needs'. The information for 2021/22 can be found at the following link:

https://www.gov.uk/government/publications/national-funding-formula-for-schools-and-high-needs

To make it easier to refer to the web pages quoted, you can download a PDF document containing clickable links at https://bit.ly/3iLEwDn.

DfE considered the pattern of LA formulae when establishing the NFF, but did not necessarily follow the national averages. They adjusted some factors to reflect political priorities such as low prior attainment and the higher costs of small rural schools.

While the Soft NFF is still in place, LA decisions on the pace at which the local formula moves towards the NFF values have to be undertaken in close consultation with their schools. These decisions partly depend on local priorities, where the starting point is, and how much money the LA receives.

One key issue can be the difference between primary and secondary per-pupil funding, which varies significantly across the country. Where the gap in NFF values is very different to the local differential, there could be a significant realignment. This could bring a reliance on transitional protection for one of the phases, as the LA moves towards or adopts the NFF values. This swing has caused some LAs to delay the change, but it will be unavoidable when the NFF is fully introduced.

Alongside the policy paper published each summer, the DfE uses the NFF to calculate an average amount per primary and secondary pupil for each LA as the basis of next year's grant. It publishes **notional** school-level allocations for mainstream schools, but there are significant caveats behind the figures. They are primarily for LA planning purposes and are based on the previous year's October census data, i.e. assuming rolls are static.

The important point is that these **notional allocations are not guaranteed**. The primary and secondary average per-pupil values for each

LA will be multiplied by the next set of October census data to create the actual Dedicated Schools Grant (DSG). LAs will then distribute this via their local formula using the new data, which is provided by the DfE.

Not only could the pupil numbers be different in the new census, but the mix of characteristics might change, affecting the distribution of funding between schools in your area. This will be true under the Hard NFF too, but your data will be compared to the national data.

While the Soft NFF is in operation, an LA can transfer money from the mainstream school pot to support a shortfall in the High Needs element of the DSG. This will reduce the amount available for the mainstream formula.

Level of funding and transition to the NFF

In response to sustained lobbying about the inadequacy of funding for schools, the government has provided some increases since the introduction of the NFF. These have been necessary in order to allow for rising rolls, improve the level of protection for schools adversely affected by the national formula, and enable under-funded schools to get to the NFF faster.

In 2021/22, the existing teachers' pay and pension increase grants are being transferred into the NFF. If you are a LA maintained school, you will not receive separate allocations for them after March 2021, and academies will receive their last separate payment in Summer 2021.

The pay grant and the per-pupil element of the pensions grant are being added to the basic entitlement (Age Weighted Pupil Unit) NFF factor in 2021/22. Allocations from the pensions Supplementary Fund will be added to core funding separately. Schools receiving protection (see below) must receive the equivalent to their 2020/21 allocations for these grants in full.

Note that the pay grant only covers the 2018 and 2019 awards; the government believes the extra funding in the settlement for 2020/21 onwards should cover the 2020 award. This won't be true for all schools, due to the redistribution involved in the NFF.

Protections

There are two main types of protection within the calculation of each LA's grant for schools. The aim is to address particular risks relating to the level of funding or changes due to the NFF:

- Minimum Per Pupil Levels (MPPL) are meant to provide a realistic amount of funding per pupil for the lowest funded schools (those with minimal additional needs). The policy paper shows the amounts for each year; the calculation includes all factors relating to pupil numbers and characteristics, the lump sum and sparsity.

- The Minimum Funding Guarantee (MFG) provides a guaranteed percentage increase in total pupil-led funding excluding lump sums and rates. It is decided afresh annually; in 2020/21 it was +1.84% and in 2021/22 +2%. But LAs can provide a lower protection level.

LAs have to pass on the MPPLs to schools in the local formula. However, they have some discretion over the MFG, should they be unable to balance the formula to the available grant. But they must choose a MFG increase within a range set by the government. In 2020/21 and 2021/22, the lowest is +0.5% and the highest is the NFF MFG level, i.e. 1.84% and 2% respectively.

Common reasons for LAs to give a lesser MFG are pressures in the High Needs Budget and historic spend items. It's also possible for the updated census data used in the formula to cause pressures, e.g. higher free school meal eligibility or lower prior attainment.

Gains due to the NFF

One other flexibility for LAs relates to the speed at which schools can gain from the NFF. The original version of the national formula limited (capped) gains in order to pay for protection. Part of the higher funding settlement from 2020/21 onwards has been used to abolish capping. This means the funding provided to LAs is sufficient **in theory** to allow all schools below the NFF to move straight on to it.

However, as explained above, there might be local circumstances which make it difficult for LAs to replicate the NFF within the available resources. Therefore they are still permitted to cap gains in the local formula if they need to. This could also happen if the protection arrangements are too costly.

The impact of pupil numbers

The information provided by the government is focused on per-pupil funding. So when considering how much cash you might receive, it's important to think about the impact of pupil numbers.

If rolls are declining, you could receive less in cash terms than in the previous year, even with static or slightly improved per pupil funding. There is a tension in the funding system: your allocation is largely based on pupil numbers, but your costs are more likely to be influenced by the number of classes you need. So falling rolls can cause a sharp drop in funding, and you will find it hard to make savings unless you can drop a class or two.

On the other hand, schools with pupil number growth should see a better cash result, because the minimum change in per pupil funding is an increase.

Of course, it's all very well getting more money for additional pupils, but the key question is how much extra you need to spend on them. Providing for them at a marginal cost could allow you to cope with a low increase, cover cost pressures or improve provision, depending on your overall situation.

Impact of the High Needs NFF on mainstream school budgets

We've already referred to one other issue which has the potential to affect the amount of funding that goes into school budget shares: pressures in spending on special educational needs and disabilities (SEND). There are elements of funding within school budget shares and academy GAG for low-level SEND, but funding for those with high needs comes from the High Needs Block of DSG. This is paid to the LA for distribution to settings, including mainstream and special schools, Pupil Referral Units/Alternative Provision settings, and independent and non-maintained special schools.

While some LAs are receiving significant increases in their High Needs allocations under the NFF, others are not. Protection has been improved recently, allowing a minimum increase of 8% per head of 2-18 population in both 2020/21 and 2021/22. However, the number of Education, Health and Care Plans (EHCPs) has risen significantly over the last two years, as have costs, so this may not be anywhere near enough for some areas.

LAs that are not receiving enough High Needs funding will need to find a way to cut costs in provision and services; many already have large deficits. This situation could affect mainstream schools in various ways, depending on their LA's response to the situation:

- An increased emphasis on inclusion, in an attempt to avoid high cost specialist provision;
- Greater challenge over whether mainstream schools are using budget share or GAG to cover the first £10k of costs for pupils with higher levels of SEND;
- Asking Schools Forums for permission to transfer up to 0.5% of the Schools Block to fund pressures in the High Needs Budget. This will reduce the amount of money available in the formula. LAs can appeal to the Secretary of State if the Forum refuses, or ask for permission to transfer more than 0.5% if Forum agrees. However, there can be a high rate of refusal by the DfE.

Will funding be enough to cover cost pressures?

A key question is whether the total amount of funding will be sufficient to cover the cost pressures that schools are collectively experiencing.

A 2019 report by the Institute of Fiscal Studies, which is summarised at https://www.ifs.org.uk/publications/14369, stated that the increased funding for schools up to 2022/23 announced in the Spending Review '*represents 7.4% expected real-terms growth in spending per pupil between 2019–20 and 2022–23 and is sufficient to almost completely reverse the cuts of 8% seen since 2009–10. If delivered, this will leave school spending per pupil in England about the same level in 2022–23 as it was in 2009–10. No real-terms growth in spending per pupil over 13 years represents a large squeeze by historical standards.*'

But this is at a national level. Individual schools won't all receive the same increase, due to the impact of the NFF and local formula decisions. We also don't know how cost pressures will develop over this period. There is no extra funding for the 2020 teachers' pay award, as there never is for the support staff award. Covid-19 could create long-term additional costs.

Another reason to be cautious about using the national cost pressure estimates is that not all schools have the same spending profile. The impact of pay-related pressures will be more severe for schools that spend a higher than average proportion of their budget on staffing. The use of pupil numbers for the pay grant and most of the pensions grant has probably created inadequate allocations for schools with high additional and special needs, due to the enhanced staffing levels they require for small groups.

The Department believes schools can still find additional savings, and has provided a suite of Resource Management tips and tools, including case studies and video clips highlighting best practice, which you can find at https://www.gov.uk/government/publications/supporting-excellent-school-resource-management.

The main areas covered are:

- Managing school workforce
- Better value procurement
- Data and transparency
- Financial skills
- Oversight, intervention and targeted support
- Improving the infrastructure of the school estate

There is also a self-assessment tool for academies at this link: https://www.gov.uk/government/publications/school-resource-management-self-assessment-tool.

Clearly, if some schools receive an increase as low as 0.5% per pupil, they will struggle to manage new pay awards and other cost pressures. Many will also find it difficult to obtain funding for pupils with SEND due to the shortfall in LA High Needs budgets. It is likely that the financial challenges will continue for some time.

How to keep informed

LAs have to perform a difficult balancing act under the Soft NFF for the reasons already outlined. They will start modelling once the notional allocations are published, which provide a firm amount per primary and secondary pupil, and can use local data on pupil numbers to estimate their Dedicated Schools Grant allocation.

However, it is only when final data is provided by the DfE and grant allocations are announced in December that affordability can be judged. There is a very tight timescale between this point and the submission of the final formula to DfE in mid-January each year.

While the LA (usually the Lead Member or equivalent for Education) takes the final decision on the local funding formula, there is a statutory requirement for them to consult all schools and academies on any significant changes to it. Whenever the move to the Hard NFF happens, the only bearing that local decisions will have is as a starting point for the calculation of whatever transitional protection the DfE deems necessary at that point.

This consultation is likely to take place during the autumn term to inform the LA's budget setting strategy. Before consulting all schools on any proposals to change the local formula, LAs will usually discuss them with the Schools Forum. Papers for Schools Forum meetings have to be published on a website, so reports to the Forum should be available for all interested parties to read.

We therefore recommend that school leaders keep an eye on the published information, and stay in touch with the Forum members who are representing them. It is often helpful to discuss proposals at network, cluster or LA-wide meetings, taking every opportunity to engage in local debates and respond to any formal consultations.

However, at the time of writing, there has been no word from DfE about any arrangements for consultation on future changes after the Hard NFF is introduced.

4 LEADING ROLES IN FINANCE

Governing Body or Board

The Governing Body or Board has first line responsibility for the resources delegated to the school. It decides the high-level vision, strategic direction and objectives to be pursued. We will use the term Board to cover the Governing Body and the academy Board of Trustees, since it is regularly used nowadays.

Strategic direction in relation to finance means that the Board plays a leading part in strategic financial leadership, ensuring resources are allocated in support of the objectives in the School Development Plan (SDP), which can also be referred to as the School Improvement Plan. Governors need to maintain a broad picture of the school's financial management and play a role in decision-making at the appropriate levels. The Board should not get involved in operational detail, unless in exceptional circumstances such as a breach of financial controls.

The most recent edition of the Governance Handbook can be found at https://www.gov.uk/government/publications/governance-handbook.

The handbook outlines three core functions for the Board, the third of which relates to finance: Overseeing the financial performance of the organisation and making sure its money is well spent. Recent versions have placed a much stronger emphasis on the link between educational and financial performance.

While the guidance states that 'It is essential that every board has at least one person with the skills to understand and interpret the full detail of the educational performance and the financial data available', it goes on to say that 'everyone on the board should be able to engage fully with discussions about data in relation to the educational and financial performance of their school'.

The Board's programme of work should include key financial aspects, with activities planned according to the financial cycle and the school's financial position. Areas would include preparation and approval of the SDP and budget, both in detail annually and in outline form for a three to five-year advance period, and deficit recovery plans if appropriate. The Board would also monitor these plans on a regular basis, to ensure progress is in line with what is expected.

The programme should also include value for money work, such as ensuring the completion and approval of the School Financial Value Standard (SFVS) for LA maintained schools and the Self-Assessment Tool for academy trusts, and receiving audit reports and internal reports where areas of the school's operation have been reviewed and recommendations made for changes.

Everything should be examined through the lens of how well outcomes for pupils have been delivered and whether the priorities approved by governors have been met. At all times, governors should also be aware of the accountability requirements on the school from external bodies, reflecting the fact that most of the funding provided to the school comes from the taxpayer.

It is the responsibility of the full Board to approve the annual budget, usually on the recommendation of the Finance Committee or equivalent. The Finance Committee should have a more thorough knowledge of financial matters; it plays an important role in challenging and developing budget proposals and budget monitoring reports throughout the year.

It can sometimes be difficult for governors to ask questions on finance, but it is critical that they do so. When stories hit the press of illegal payments or misuse of school funding, members of staff or unknown fraudsters are sometimes able to get away with such misdemeanours as a result of ineffective oversight and challenge by governors. When a set of information is presented, it is important to have governors with critical thinking and analytical skills to interpret it and ask perceptive questions.

It can also be difficult for a Board to deny requests by senior leaders for pay increases where insufficient supporting evidence has been provided, but part of the responsibility for achieving value for money lies in ensuring all expenditure is fully justified and that there is a return on any additional investment.

Newer governors in particular may be hesitant about asking finance-related questions at meetings, for fear of wasting the time of more experienced members of the Board. However, it will often come as a relief to others who have been wondering about that very issue but didn't dare speak out! A good Chair of Governors will encourage questioning and will support governors in building up their confidence to challenge areas that don't seem quite right.

Given all of the above, you can see that finance is an area where it is absolutely essential for governors to keep up to date, especially when funding reforms are in progress. Training may be available within the school, delivered by the School Business Leader or MAT Chief Financial Officer, or alternatively it could be purchased from local authorities and external providers. It should not only be taken up by new governors but also by those who are more experienced. School finance and funding matters change so quickly that it is easy for anyone to lose track.

The Governance Handbook provides some helpful prompts for questions on financial matters, and indicates where you can find financial data and tools to help judge whether a school is delivering value for money and suggest areas for informed questioning. There is also a specific guide for governors and trustees on understanding your data, with a useful Annex A that includes key financial themes for governors to consider, available at

https://www.gov.uk/government/publications/understanding-your-data-a-guide-for-school-governors-and-academy-trustees.

The DfE's school resource management web pages also provide advice and guidance. The 'Top Ten Planning Checks for Governors' is a particularly helpful document, providing a set of questions to determine if value for money is being achieved. It has a strong focus on staffing and contractual payments. The guidance can be found at:

https://www.gov.uk/guidance/school-resource-management-top-10-planning-checks-for-governors.

Headteacher

The headteacher is responsible for implementing the decisions of the Board. This usually means taking delegated responsibility for operational management, for example decision-making on staffing and resources.

Every school should have a Scheme of Delegation which outlines the financial limits for the headteacher to take decisions on expenditure without consulting governors. This should be reviewed from time to time, to make sure it reflects the reality of day-to-day management requirements and the level of trust and responsibility invested in the headteacher by the governors. The financial limits should be high enough to prevent leaders having to go to governors too frequently with requests to purchase essential items, while making sure there is sufficient oversight of costly decisions that could pose a risk to the budget.

Communication between the headteacher and Chair of Governors is critically important, particularly in the area of finance. Governors must receive financial information that is relevant, timely, accurate and at an appropriate level to provide assurance that resources are being well used and that there is a high level of financial control. It is important that the information is provided well before the meeting, allowing time for it to be read and understood. Any unusual features, for example large variances in budget monitoring reports, should be highlighted, with supporting information to help governors to understand the implications.

The headteacher should expect to be challenged on any financial information presented to governors, and should ensure that they can provide a professional response. If the School Business Leader is not going to be present at a Board or Finance Committee meeting, they will usually be able to provide background working papers if required. If a headteacher is not confident of the answer, it is better to agree to provide information after the meeting, rather than guess.

On occasions, the headteacher may feel that governors are straying into operational detail. Sometimes this may manifest itself in a parent governor bringing personal issues into meetings, for example about their own child, or a staff governor trying to exert their influence on an internal management matter.

The best way of dealing with this is usually to consult the Chair of Governors, who can steer governors appropriately. Sometimes it may be necessary for the Chair to address the matter privately with any particular governor who is making unreasonable demands. As already mentioned, a programme of work should be in place which will generally make clear the sort of areas which governors are entitled to examine.

5 AN OVERVIEW OF THE SCHOOL BUDGETING PROCESS

Legal requirements

What are the legal requirements and expectations on a school in terms of budgeting and managing the use of its resources? They can be summarised in two key duties:

- Set a balanced budget within the available resources;
- Comply with the requirements set by your funding body: the local authority for LA maintained schools (including Foundation Trust schools) or the Education and Skills Funding Agency (ESFA) for academies and free schools.

Funding body requirements cover a wide range of detailed financial matters such as internal control, assets, debts, financial systems, monitoring information provided to the funding body, treatment of income, and audit arrangements. In this chapter, we will focus on setting a budget within the available resources, but you will see some references to the requirements of funding bodies as they relate to the preparation of a budget.

Setting a balanced revenue budget

This book focuses on preparation and monitoring of a revenue budget, which covers ongoing operational expenditure to run the regular activities of the school. Capital budgets tend to work differently according to the funding source, and can straddle more than one financial year.

The basic requirement for a school is to set a balanced revenue budget. This means planning your spending within the limits of the resources available to the school. It isn't restricted to the income and expenditure within a single year; the definition of 'balanced' includes any unspent balances or deficit carried forward from previous years.

Most schools will aim to hold a small contingency in case of unexpected problems, since things don't always work out in line with your plans at the start of the year. Keeping a modest reserve for this purpose is sensible resource management.

The requirement for a balanced budget is covered in the main compliance documents published by the funding bodies:

- Local Authorities will have a section in the Scheme for Financing Schools which requires schools to approve a balanced budget and to submit this to the LA once approved. They will also request regular monitoring reports which include a forecast of the year end position.
- The Academies Financial Handbook states: 'The board of trustees **must** approve a balanced budget, and any significant changes to it, for the financial year to 31 August, which can draw on unspent funds brought forward from previous years. The board **must** minute its approval.'

Following a consultation on financial transparency in 2019, in July 2020 the DfE introduced a directed revision to LA Schemes for Financing Schools, to require all schools to submit a three-year budget forecast each year from 2021/22. Academies had previously been required to do the same, and many LAs had already expected their schools to submit forecasts. This provides a medium-term context, and your annual budgets over this period should work towards the end point, although it will naturally be amended as it rolls forward.

You must set a budget that you are confident of achieving. Knowingly overstating income budgets or understating expenditure budgets, aware they can't be achieved, would breach the requirement to balance the budget. This is an area where it's important for governors to challenge senior leaders.

The ability of schools to carry unspent balances forward allows expenditure to be spread over more than one year. While all schools need some working balances, this is particularly useful for LA maintained schools, whose financial year starts in April and therefore doesn't match up with the academic year beginning in September. The ESFA year for post 16 funding is different again, starting in July, but let's not go into that!

However, if you'll forgive the pun, you have to strike a balance when it comes to holding surpluses. Whilst a deficit should be strenuously avoided, stockpiling of excessive balances is just as undesirable. The funding you are given in a particular year is intended to be spent on the pupils that are currently in school.

This plays out in various ways; for example, parents would be very concerned if they knew that their child wasn't receiving their entitlement, and the level of balances can also influence politicians and decision-makers when responding to the education sector's concerns about the level of funding. We will go into more detail about school balances and their use later in this book.

Deficits

It is illegal to set a deficit budget, i.e. one that is not balanced to the available funding including any surpluses or deficits brought forward, unless you have approval from your funding body. A deficit budget would technically require a school to borrow money, which is not permitted. As we've already noted, the funding body is the LA for maintained schools, and the ESFA for academies.

We could wait to discuss this topic until after we've shown you how to construct your budget. But it's better to understand the implications of a potential deficit before you go through the process. It will provide an extra motivation for your efforts to balance the budget.

So, what is the process that you need to follow if you can't keep within the available funding for next year's budget? Firstly, the obvious advice is to re-examine everything in detail to check for any errors and try to identify sufficient savings to balance it. This book is intended to provide prompts to help you with these checks and budget balancing, but our companion volume 'Leading a School Budget Review' goes into much greater depth on the subject.

If you are absolutely sure the budget still can't be balanced for the year in question, you must notify your funding body. This applies even if you know you can resolve it in the following year; the test applies to each annual budget.

There are different arrangements for LA maintained schools and academies in this situation. Let's look at LA maintained schools first.

Process for LA schools needing a Licensed Deficit

An LA maintained school that is unable to balance its budget must apply to the LA for a Licensed Deficit. This gives you permission to set a deficit budget. From the LA's point of view, the deficit will be offset against the balances of other maintained schools held by them. The local Scheme for Financing Schools will contain a section outlining the process to be followed.

The LA will usually ask the school to provide a three-year budget projection and any relevant background information. It will normally arrange a meeting with the headteacher and chair of governors before a decision is taken on whether to approve a Licensed Deficit or not.

The Licensed Deficit can only operate for a limited time, after which the school will be expected to have achieved a balanced budget. The DfE's statutory guidance for Schemes states that the maximum length over which a school may repay the deficit should not exceed three years, with appropriate mechanisms to ensure deficits are not extended indefinitely.

As part of the process, a school will be asked to produce a formal recovery plan. There will usually be monitoring meetings with officers from the LA to check that progress is being made in achieving the plan. If approval is not given for a Licensed Deficit, the school has to bring the budget back into balance before the year end. LAs can set an upper limit for the amount they are prepared to license. If the deficit breaches this, the LA might not approve the full amount, in which case further savings will have to be found immediately, to reduce the deficit to the level that is approved.

Conditions may be attached to the approval, depending on the LA's level of confidence in the school's ability to set and achieve the recovery plan. The school needs to display an awareness of why there is a deficit and should be able to inspire confidence in its ability to get the budget back on track within the agreed time period.

Withdrawal of delegation from LA maintained schools

Depending on LA officers' views about the school's capacity to improve their financial arrangements, the LA has the option of withdrawing delegation. This may happen if monitoring reports during the period of the Licensed Deficit show that the school is not on track to get back into balance.

Withdrawal of delegation means that decision-making on financial matters is surrendered to the LA, and the school loses control. This is usually regarded as a last resort by the LA, because it has very little spare capacity to manage individual schools. It is also undesirable for a school to be relieved of its responsibility to sort out the deficit that it has itself generated. It's too easy for governors and leaders to blame the LA if decisions on spending lead to a decline in standards.

Nevertheless, officers may feel that withdrawing delegation is unavoidable if there is little prospect of the school adhering to the recovery plan, especially if there are also performance issues which could result in a poor Ofsted judgement, intervention by DfE and enforced academisation. The LA has to write off any deficit if that happens; withdrawing delegation therefore represents an attempt to stop a deficit escalating out of control. However, a deficit for a school that voluntarily converts transfers to the academy.

Since the LA is responsible for ensuring school improvement, it can also withdraw delegation if an increasing deficit is judged to have an adverse impact on teaching and learning and therefore on outcomes for pupils.

It is difficult to appreciate the impact that withdrawal of delegation might have until it happens, but it is generally a most unsatisfactory position to be in from the school's perspective, as well as that of the local authority. It can cause paralysis in decision-making, as everything has to be agreed by the LA. The school will have to make requests for new expenditure, justifying why it is necessary. Existing commitments will be examined to see if the expenditure can be avoided, and the ability to replace staff who leave is not guaranteed.

Process for academy trusts in deficit

The Academies Financial Handbook says: 'The board of trustees must notify ESFA within 14 calendar days of its meeting if proposing to set a deficit revenue budget for the current financial year, which it cannot address after taking into account unspent funds from previous years.'

The risk is greater for a single academy trust than in a MAT, because the focus is on the trust as the legal entity. If the trust has a reasonable surplus, the DfE is less concerned about individual academy deficits within a MAT.

A MAT collects the General Annual Grant (GAG) allocations for its academies and can pool them at trust level then redistribute the money to fund specific priorities within the trust. This means the trust can take proactive action to address a deficit in one or more of its academies by redirecting resources for a period of time, in addition to any top-slicing of grant for central services provided by the trust.

The national redistribution of funding caused by the National Funding Formula could cause some debates about this matter, because moving money within a MAT can be a difficult thing to do if the budgets for most of the academies in it are particularly challenging.

The NFF has not affected the ability of a MAT to pool GAG. This is surprising, because it runs counter to the NFF principle of consistency in funding for similar schools and will prevent the achievement of a true NFF.

Because of this flexibility, the DfE expects a MAT to act quickly to tackle deficits in individual academies, potentially using centrally-held reserves or adjusting other academies' funding. A recovery plan should be put in place to avoid a permanent transfer. In essence, this is similar to the LA system of

Licensed Deficits, underwritten from the surpluses of other schools. But in the academy system, cash flow also has to be considered.

Financial Notice to Improve

The main mechanism the ESFA uses to tackle academy deficits is a Financial Notice to Improve (FNtI). This is not the only reason a Notice can be issued; they are also used where there are concerns about financial management or governance. These could include cash flow problems, risk of insolvency, irregular use of public funds, weak oversight and control by trustees, and breaches of the rules on related party transactions.

FNtIs are published by the DfE, so anyone can read them. You can see them at https://www.gov.uk/government/collections/academies-financial-notices-to-improve; note that they are in alphabetical order, not by date.

The Academies Financial Handbook makes it clear that if an FNtI is issued to a trust, the ESFA will automatically withdraw delegated authorities and other freedoms. The Handbook lists the transactions which must be approved in advance by ESFA. The impact of withdrawing delegation is therefore similar for both LA schools and academies.

Once the terms set out in the FNtI have been complied with, and the ESFA judges that improvement is sustainable, delegated authorities will be returned to the academy. The withdrawal of an FNtI is also published on the Gov.uk website.

The ultimate sanction if the academy does not comply with the requirements of the Notice is a transfer of the academy to another Academy Trust, or the withdrawal of the funding agreement, leading to closure. This has happened; it is not an idle threat.

Delegated and Devolved Funding

The school budget must account for how you will spend all the funding received, whether it is delegated or devolved. It's therefore important to be clear about the difference between these two types of funding.

Delegated funding

The most obvious example of delegated funding is the school's budget share, or in the case of academies, the equivalent element of General Annual Grant (GAG). The responsibility for deciding how to spend it is delegated to the Board. In turn, as we've already seen, governors can delegate some of this responsibility to the headteacher, up to a maximum threshold. Delegated funding may be spent on anything as long as it is legal, without having to ask permission from the body which provided the funding.

Sometimes the government may change its mind about what is legal. For example, in the past the school budget share could only be spent on the children on roll in that school. Separate funding was given for community activities and this had to be accounted for separately. But later these rules were relaxed; budget share can now be used in collaborative arrangements, even where it benefits children who don't attend the school. This change meant schools no longer had to navigate complicated accounting arrangements for community activities.

Your annual funding statement shows the characteristics of your school and its pupils together with the funding allocated across various factors, e.g. basic entitlement, free school meal (FSM) pupils, low prior attainment, pupils with English as an Additional Language and pupil mobility. This tells you how funding has been distributed between the schools in the area, but you are free to spend it however you wish. For example, you are not restricted to spending only the amount shown for FSM on eligible pupils; you can spend more or less on them, or you can spend it on other pupils. However, if particular groups of pupils do not make progress, you may be asked to justify your decisions at the next inspection.

Your core funding (budget share or the equivalent in GAG) only covers funding for Reception to Year 11 provision. Funding for early years and post-16 provision is also delegated. This means you don't have to spend each pot of money only on the purposes for which it is given (which would be referred to as ring fencing the money). You can combine the funding and spend it however you wish. This means there is nothing to prevent you from cross-subsidising costs between the main school and nursery or sixth form (depending on the school's age range), except of course a general shortage of funding.

Devolved funding

Sometimes a school will receive devolved funding, usually in the form of specific grants such as Pupil Premium and Primary PE & Sport grants. Unlike delegated funding, you are required to spend this on the specific purpose for which each grant is given.

It is important to be aware of the rules for each grant, as there can be different restrictions. Sometimes a certain amount of 'leakage' is permitted, which means that while delivering the activity that the grant is intended for, some other pupils may benefit from it. But care must be taken to limit this to a minor benefit, so as not to breach the terms of the grant. The gov.uk website provides guidance on the terms and conditions of government grants.

If you have other specific grants, you should have documentation that makes clear the basis on which funding has been awarded.

Approaches to budget preparation

Approaches to budget preparation generally range between two extremes: zero based budgeting and incremental budgeting.

Zero based budgeting

A zero based approach means that the budget is created from scratch, starting with a blank sheet and building up the requirements. A new school will have to do this, and may talk to other similar schools to get a sense of the likely costs for some functions. It's a bit like moving into a new house and not knowing how much it costs to run.

A school in financial difficulty could also choose to adopt this method, rejecting previous patterns of expenditure and building up the allocation of money to activities (known as cost centres) from scratch. Various techniques can be used to establish appropriate limits on expenditure. Most of your budget should be based on priorities, using the School Development Plan.

Zero based budgeting helps you focus on your priorities. You will need to reflect your school operations in financial terms, challenging whether expenditure is essential or not and taking curriculum planning into account. It helps you avoid falling into the trap of assuming that you need a particular level of budget just because you spent that much in a previous year.

However, this approach is also very time consuming, and in an ongoing situation the difference it makes may not be worth the effort. If significant savings have to be made, a fundamental budget review is the best approach, as outlined in our book 'Leading a School Budget Review'. This will enable you to keep the current level of funding for areas you are confident in, and focus your efforts on areas where you are not achieving value for money.

Incremental budgeting

The incremental approach is more straightforward, involving simply rolling forward the previous year's budget. There will be some adjustments needed, such as for pay awards, any changes in employment costs (national insurance and pensions), and inflation on non-pay expenditure.

The main advantages of this approach are simplicity and speed. As long as your internal controls are effective, most spending won't vary significantly from the previous year and will only require a small adjustment.

However, remember to check whether activity levels have changed, and amend your budget lines accordingly if needed. You should also ensure that changes in priorities are reflected, so that the budget delivers the vision.

Another disadvantage of the incremental approach is that it can easily tempt you into the practice of 'adding a bit' for headings such as repairs and maintenance or educational resources where there is a wide choice in what is spent. This poses a greater risk of a shortfall when it is all added up and compared to the available funding. You might then have to go back to the drawing board and start reviewing individual areas to find savings.

Which to choose?

In practice, most schools take an approach somewhere between zero-based and incremental budgeting, according to their circumstances. The key question is what financial commitments have been made in compiling the SDP; these will need to be reflected in the budget, with a check to make sure that the costings for key initiatives and priorities are accurate.

For areas that are most likely to change, such as staffing in a large school, it is safest to build up those budget lines from scratch, based on a stated set of assumptions. We will go into this in more detail in later chapters.

For most of the non-pay headings, subject to what we've said about the SDP and other priorities, it's more likely that most of the previous year's budget can be rolled forward with minor adjustments. The estimated year-end result for the current year (also known as a predicted outturn) may show some variations in actual expenditure compared to the budget, and you will need to decide whether to make adjustments in the new year.

Some current year variances might be one-off in nature, due to a particular issue, such as emergency repairs to the building or unusually high levels of maternity leave. Where it is an adverse variance which could be attributed to poor control by a budget holder, you will want to avoid rewarding their overspending. Conversely, it is not desirable to penalise someone who has not fully spent their budget, by adjusting the following year's allocation downwards to achieve a permanent saving.

Each area needs to be considered on its own merits, in consultation with budget holders and senior leaders, and a decision needs to be taken on the best approach. For example, you could consider the impact of trends in energy consumption and prices. The need for educational resources can be assessed for a given number of pupils or in response to curriculum changes.

You might decide that in areas such as IT consumables, printing and stationery, staff can be expected to manage within a fixed budget or even a slightly reduced budget to encourage them to make efficiency savings. These are defined as the trimming of costs without any adverse impact on outcomes (what is achieved with the spending). You may find that priorities have changed and new initiatives need to be funded.

The ultimate aim is to set a balanced budget that is realistic, will allow you to deliver the school's vision within the available resources, and represents value for money.

Later we will talk about a strategic financial plan which acts as a blueprint for your priorities, showing how you will allocate resources over the next three to five years. But first we will focus on annual budget preparation, on the assumption that such a strategic financial plan is already in place.

The budget cycle

There is an annual budget cycle which every school goes through in order to achieve a balanced budget in time for the start of the financial year. It won't come as a surprise to hear that we advocate the linking of the budget cycle with the school educational planning cycle.

This cycle differs slightly for schools and academies, according to their different financial years: April to March for LA maintained schools and September to August for academies. Below we suggest examples of the cycle for each; these may vary depending on local circumstances and sources of information, but should be broadly compatible with what is expected.

DfE publishes a timeline for schools and academies, but sometimes they are taken offline for updating, so you will need to search for the most up to date versions. You should keep an eye on these for any changes.

Firstly we will outline the budget cycle for an LA maintained school, then the subsequent table will cover it for an academy. In both cases we show the school planning cycle alongside, which is the same for both because it covers the academic year.

1. LA Maintained School Budget Planning Cycle

Month	**School Planning Cycle:** (all schools)	**Budget Planning Cycle:** LA Maintained School – year end 31 March
September	• Whole School SEF completed. • Whole School Development Plan completed (start date from 1 September). Presented to GB in autumn term	• Start gathering information for the following financial year (7 months from now).
October	• Faculty Development Plans completed. • Curriculum lesson modelling and staffing forecasting.	• October census informs school funding – ensure accuracy. • Ensure you understand your school context/data profile and how this may be changing. • Undertake an early estimate of available funding for the following financial year. • Prepare current year outturn predictions. Continue on at least a monthly basis until finalised.
November		• Watch out for Schools Forum decisions, including the LA's budget strategy. • Update current year outturn prediction.
December	• Dec/Jan Options process begins for secondary schools.	• Update current year outturn prediction. • Review services, contracts and buybacks, giving sufficient time to make appropriate changes before renewal. • Undertake financial benchmarking as part of your budget planning and review.

January		• Start detailed salary forecasts, updating them regularly.
February	• Review of Whole School SEF, Whole School Development Plan and Faculty Development Plans.	• Confirmation of funding from LA. • Discussion with budget holders on their requirements for the following year, from SDP reviews (SLT level and individual budget holders). • Preparation for year-end work. • Update current year outturn prediction.
March		• Compare your original funding estimate to new school budget share information and adjust. • Financial year-end work. • Provisional budget presented and submitted. • Latest date to submit SFVS (can be at any date in year) including evidence of SDP link to budget. • Update current year outturn prediction to be presented as provisional outturn. Start to plan use of balances.
April	• Gather information on applications for following September intake. • Options requests to be received by Easter. • Staffing allocation planning begins.	• New budget year begins. • Check receipt of nursery funding allocations compared to your early estimates throughout the year as in-year adjustments are made. • Finalise outturn prediction for previous year. • Undertake a self-assessment of internal controls and present Statement of Internal Control (SIC) to governors (at any time after the year-end).

May	• Review and update of Whole School SEF, Whole School Development Plan and Faculty Development Plans. • Timetabling scheduling and construction begins.	
June		• Finalise previous year outturn prediction and confirm planned use of balances. • Compare actual Pupil Premium funding allocation to your early estimate and update budget. • Final budget presented to GB and submitted to LA in line with timescale in local Scheme for Financing Schools. • Final outturn position, planned use of balances and Statement of Internal Control (SIC) presented to LA.
July	• Final deadline for timetables for following September to be completed and communicated to staff.	
August		
September	• Whole School SEF completed. • Whole School Development Plan completed (start date 1 Sep). Presented to GB in autumn term.	• Start gathering information for the following financial year.

2. Academy Budget Planning Cycle

Month	School Planning Cycle: (all schools)	Budget Planning Cycle: Academy – year end 31 August
September	• Whole School SEF completed. • Whole School Development Plan completed (start date from 1 September). Presented to GB in autumn term	• Start preparing information for auditors to feed into final accounts, audited in autumn term and submitted by 31 Dec • New budget year begins • Check receipt of nursery funding allocations compared to your early estimates throughout the year, as in-year adjustments are made. • Start gathering information for the following financial year (12 months from now).
October	• Faculty Development Plans completed. • Curriculum lesson modelling and staffing forecasting.	• October census informs school funding – ensure accuracy. If you are funded on estimated rolls, ensure there is a dialogue with the ESFA. • Ensure you understand your school context/data profile and how this may be changing. • Undertake an early estimate of available funding for the following financial year. • Complete land and buildings collection tool (delayed in 2020/21 due to Covid; normally submitted early November.
November		• Final accounts to be audited prior to 31 December ESFA submission deadline. • Feedback from Audit/Trustees report to local governing boards for previous year's accounts. • Watch out for Schools Forum decisions, including the LA's

		budget strategy, as this will also have an impact on academy funding distribution.
December	• Dec/Jan Options process begins for secondary schools.	Submit to the ESFA by 31 December: • a copy of the audited accounts, including the reporting accountant's report on regularity. • a copy of the auditor's management letter. • an accounts submission cover (on-line form). Accounts include: Reports • a trustees' report • a governance statement • a statement on regularity, propriety and compliance • a statement of trustees' responsibilities • an independent auditor's report on the financial statements • an independent reporting accountant's assurance report on regularity Financial statements • a statement of financial activities ('SOFA') • a balance sheet • a statement of cash flows • notes which expand on the statements
January		• Submit Accounts return to ESFA by around 19 January (see Accounts direction for relevant year). • Publication of accounts on

		trust's website by 31 January (retain for two years).
February	• Review of Whole School SEF, Whole School SDP and Faculty Development Plans.	• Confirmation of funding from ESFA – deadline is end of February.
March		• Compare early funding estimate to your funding information from ESFA; make adjustments. • Indicative budget setting arrangements for following financial year reported to local governing boards.
April	• Gather information on applications for following September intake. • Options requests to be received by Easter. • Staffing allocation planning begins.	• Review services, contracts and buybacks within sufficient time to make appropriate changes before renewal. • Undertake financial benchmarking as part of your budget planning and review. • Start detailed salary forecasts, updating regularly.
May	• Review and update of Whole School SEF, Whole School Development Plan and Faculty Development Plans. • Timetabling scheduling and construction begins.	• Submit Budget forecast return outturn to ESFA by around 18 May (see accounts direction for relevant year). • Discussion with budget holders on their requirements for the following year – from development plan reviews (SLT level and individual budget holders). • Previous year accounts filed with Companies House by 31 May.
June		• Check receipt of Pupil Premium funding allocation compared to your early estimate and update budget. • Consideration and approval of

		draft budget for next financial year to local governing boards. • Arrangements for external auditor for autumn term to be considered by governing board.
July	• Final deadline for timetables for following September to be completed and communicated to staff.	• Submit budget forecast return to ESFA by end of July. • Financial year end work. • Start to plan use of balances.
August		• Financial year-end work. • Plan use of balances. *be aware of holiday working arrangements including annual leave and plan July and August accordingly.
September	• Whole School SEF completed. • Whole School Development Plan completed (start date from 1 Sep). Presented to GB in autumn term.	• Start preparing information for auditors to feed into final accounts, audited in autumn term and submitted by 31 Dec • New budget year begins • Check receipt of nursery funding allocations compared to your early estimates throughout the year as in-year adjustments are made. • Start gathering information for the following financial year.

Timely preparation of a budget is very important. It needs to be ready at the start of the financial year, because if your budget holders don't have confirmation of their allocations at this point, they may make their own assumptions on how much money they have to spend. Staff could commit too much expenditure during the summer term, in readiness for September.

If you wait too long to start preparing your budget, you might discover at a very late stage that it doesn't balance. This could cause difficulties if you don't have sufficient time to check the figures, identify savings, re-examine priorities and discuss the revised proposals with senior leaders and governors.

Even if your school is likely to benefit from the introduction of the National Funding Formula, you could struggle to set a balanced budget because the cost pressures could outweigh the extra funding. Schools spending a high proportion of the budget on pay are most at risk.

Alternatively, you could be facing challenges in maintaining standards of attainment and progress, requiring extra support for particular groups of pupils. Your school might be experiencing growth in pupil numbers. You need to be clear on what additional staffing and resources are required.

We therefore advise you to gather together as much relevant information as you can at the earliest possible point. This will help you to make a first pass at the budget and assess whether you are likely to have enough funding to balance it. Then you will be able to work out solutions in consultation with relevant staff in time to meet the deadlines.

Having all your information to hand at an earlier point will also help to avoid delays if relevant staff are absent or cannot spare time to respond to questions. These problems somehow seem more likely to occur when you are pressed for time!

In our next chapter, we look at the first stage of your detailed budget preparation, which is the task of defining the funding that is available to your school, so that you have a target figure to balance to.

6 AVAILABLE REVENUE FUNDING

Types of funding

The first step in the actual preparation of your budget is to assess how much funding you are likely to have for the financial year in question. This chapter provides an overview of the funding elements that need to be taken into account when balancing your budget.

In summary, the main categories of revenue funding are:

- School budget share for LA maintained schools or the equivalent element of General Annual Grant (GAG) for academies;
- Pupil Premium: for Early Years, Disadvantage, Service Children and Looked After Children/care leavers/adopted children;
- Early Years Single Funding Formula from the LA for your nursery;
- Specific grants for areas such as Primary PE & Sport, Universal Infant Free School Meals etc.;
- Post-16 funding from ESFA for sixth form provision;
- SEN funding for individual children whose total costs exceed £10,000 per year, or where the notional amount of funding within budget share is proven to be insufficient to cover lower level SEND because the school is particularly inclusive;
- Grants for the teachers' pay award and pension increase (transferred into budget share/GAG from 2021/22);
- Other academy funding, e.g. Education Services Grant protection (now tapered to zero or a minimal amount for prior recipients), MAT growth funding, Start Up grant, and Post Opening Grant.

Revenue funding from all known sources should be used as the basis for your budget, to identify the figure you are trying to balance to. The vast majority of your funding is driven by pupil numbers and characteristics (over 90% nationally). In the early stages of budget preparation, you can try to make a rough prediction of your total funding using pupil numbers, if actual figures are not available. Our book 'Forecasting Mainstream School Funding' provides a step-by-step guide to this.

It is best to err on the low side when estimating funding, rather than face a shortfall. However, if you subsequently struggle to balance the budget, you will want to revisit your assumptions to make sure it's not too low, to avoid rushing into any unnecessary decisions, particularly staffing reductions.

Don't forget to check all your funding statements to ensure that there are no errors. Are your data correct and are they reflected accurately in the statement? Has your funding body provided a clear explanation of how the funding is calculated, and is it easy to understand? If not, get in touch with them and ask for further information until you are confident that it is correct.

The format of school budget share statements varies between LAs, but all should show the number of eligible pupils and the unit value for each factor in the local formula, plus any lump sums. They should also provide statements for other sources of funding such as Early Years. The GAG statement from ESFA has a standard format.

Timing of other funding streams

You will need to keep your funding allocations under review throughout the year, as some funding streams are not notified to local authorities by the government until part way through the year.

For example, **Pupil Premium** allocations to individual schools in the area are usually published in June, because they are based on eligible children who were on your roll in the January census. This is different to budget share and academy GAG, which use the previous October census. Depending on how the funding is allocated, you can use relevant data from the current year and adjust for any known changes.

The latest information and funding rates can be found on the gov.uk website at this link: https://www.gov.uk/government/publications/pupil-premium/pupil-premium.

Taking an LA school as an example, to estimate Pupil Premium for a future year, you could take the latest Ever 6 Free School Meals data as a starting point. This comprises pupils on roll in January who were eligible for FSM at any point in the last 6 years' census returns. You would then adjust it to remove leavers and add eligible starters since the relevant January census, depending on the time of year you are creating your forecasts. Anyone who was in the previous Ever 6 list will automatically be eligible as long as they are still on your roll and haven't been eligible for longer than six years. You don't need to worry about changes in rolls in September, because the January data provides the Pupil Premium funding for the whole financial year.

Watch Pupil Premium eligibility carefully; it can be affected by benefit changes or unusual events such as Coronavirus. In the past, the government has established some transitional arrangements, for example to accommodate the impact of Universal Credit roll out.

Make sure you don't double count a pupil eligible for the Deprivation Pupil Premium who is also Looked After or adopted from care; they only receive the higher rate of the Looked After Pupil Premium Plus, not both.

You also need to know whether you receive the full Pupil Premium for a Looked After Child or care leaver, or whether the LA top-slices part of the Looked After Pupil Premium for coordinated central support, which is a decision taken by the Head of the Virtual School.

Early years funding is initially a provisional allocation based on data from the January in the calendar year before the budget year (for example January 2020 for the 2021/22 budget). It is then adjusted throughout the year on the basis of actual participation, usually at termly census points.

You are safe to include the provisional allocation in your budget, in the knowledge that if nursery rolls rise, your funding will be adjusted upwards. However, if numbers go down, you will have to repay the excess funding. Make sure you understand the method and timing of adjustments made by your LA, and reserve money for any claw back of grant.

Additional **SEND funding** (for higher-level special educational needs and disabilities) is awarded separately by the LA, and it depends on the needs of individual pupils. This is referred to as 'top up funding' because it tops up the money in your budget share that is notionally designated as SEND funding to cover the first £10,000 of total costs for each pupil with high needs. A minority of pupils will need top ups. While the notional element within budget share stays with a school for use across all pupils with SEND, top up funding moves with the pupil if they transfer to another school.

SEND funding will probably be fairly stable where you have top ups from the LA for pupils with Education Health and Care Plans (EHCPs) who are continuing in school. If an annual review specifies that a pupil's needs have changed, the top up value may be adjusted. Remember to remove the top up for leavers from your estimates.

If you have referred a pupil for assessment, but no decision has yet been taken about whether they will receive an EHCP, it is probably best to be cautious and wait until the process is concluded before entering the funding. If your budget is tight, you could omit the potential funding and the cost of the support (staffing and other resources), but it is better to include estimates of both, and adjust this if necessary when a decision is reached.

The important thing is to be clear about whether both sides are included or not. If you have been able to factor in the extra expenditure, and can balance the budget without adding in the anticipated top up income for new EHCPs, any allocation subsequently received will provide some flexibility.

If you have places in SEN units or resource bases, you should be notified of the number of places being funded. The pupils occupying places in units and resource bases are counted in budget share/GAG, and you will also receive place-led funding from the LA or ESFA of £6,000. This is based on a broad assumption of an average £4,000 in your core funding, to reach the £10k threshold. However, if places are unoccupied, the lack of budget share or GAG for them means your funding body is required to pay the full £10,000 per empty place. As before, the LA will decide top up values for costs above the amount received in budget share and place-led funding.

Time limited grants

Be aware of any specific grants that are time-limited, and make sure you remove them from your total funding figure when they are about to cease. You should have a clear exit strategy in place. Ideally, staff employed as a direct result of the grant will have time-limited contracts, although they may be entitled to redundancy payments. Take HR advice on this.

Above all, you need to stop expenditure as soon as the grant ceases, unless you have secured alternative funding or governors agree the activities are important and must be built into the ongoing budget as a priority. In the latter case, you may need to make compensating savings elsewhere, in order to balance the budget.

Restrictions on in-year allocations

The bulk of your funding will be in budget share (LA schools) or General Annual Grant (academy GAG); this is fixed at the start of the year and cannot be changed except in specific cases which we outline below.

The local authority may identify an underspend in centrally held budgets at the end of the previous year. This will be confirmed when the accounts have been closed, usually in May or June.

However, a surplus can't be given out to schools once the current year's budget shares have been notified. This is because the ESFA cannot replicate any extra allocation to give a similar sum to academies. The surplus has to be held back until the following year's budget, when a decision can be taken on how to use it, e.g. to increase budget shares or support pressures in the High Needs Budget for SEND.

There are only a few exceptions to this restriction: allocations and adjustments for early years and SEND, and some centrally held funds, approved by the Schools Forum, which we will now explain.

Some local authorities have these specific central funds, but not all do; they depend on local circumstances and priorities. You should be able to see Schools Forum reports on a public website which show approval being given for these funds. If your school is eligible for them, you will be notified, or you will have made an application and know that it has been successful.

Growth Fund

Normally there is a delay in funding for ordinary changes in rolls, because core funding is based on the previous October census. This means that if your school has some additional pupils at the start of the new academic year in September, you will not usually receive funding for them until the following April if you are an LA maintained school. The delay can be a whole year if you are an academy, unless your funding is based on estimated rolls, in which case an adjustment is made later, to reflect actual numbers. On the other hand, if pupils leave, budget share and GAG are not adjusted, so for minor ups and downs this system is generally acceptable.

The situation is different if schools are asked by their LA to create an extra class, e.g. to cater for population growth or meet the infant class size rules. The normal time delay would mean many schools would struggle to subsidise additional expenditure on this sort of scale. LAs are therefore permitted to hold funding for a Growth Fund. In 2019/20 a new formula factor was created in the NFF, based on the growth in pupil numbers (ignoring falling rolls) between the latest census and the year before. For 2021/22, the comparison is between October 2019 and 2020 census data.

If the LA has a Growth Fund, it will provide additional funding to schools with roll increases above a threshold, usually on condition that these arise in response to basic need in an area. This means that the local authority has asked the school to increase its Published Admission Number (PAN) in order to meet local demand for school places. The fund isn't for popularity growth.

The Growth Fund criteria should be published on your Schools Forum website. LA Place Planning officers will usually be able to advise if your school will qualify, and provide an estimate of the additional funding which you can build into your budget. The method for calculating allocations can vary, e.g. lump sums or an amount per additional pupil or class.

Growth funding has to be made available to schools and academies on an equal basis. The exception is where academies or free schools are adding year groups, because they already receive funding from ESFA to recognise this.

If the growth is significant and likely to be permanent, LAs can decide to adjust the pupil numbers in the census to let additional funding flow through the funding formula, rather than use the Growth Fund. This will allow the pupils to attract all elements of funding rather than the more limited scope that is usually awarded through the Growth Fund.

Falling Rolls Fund

This is another discretionary fund, but its use has declined in recent years after the DfE transferred the money for it into the growth factor in the NFF. It recognises that some good or outstanding schools may have temporary falling rolls at such a level that it may be difficult to provide the required curriculum without becoming unviable.

Normally, such a school would be a candidate for closure, but the LA may know from its place planning that the empty places will be needed in the next few years to cope with anticipated pupil number growth. It would not be cost-effective to close a school, with all the costs and disruption involved, only to open a new one a couple of years later.

In these circumstances, the LA may award temporary funding to the school, based on criteria such as how under-subscribed the school is and the extent of the shortfall. DfE have set a condition that only good or outstanding schools are eligible. The fund cannot be used to compensate for loss of funding due to formula changes or inefficiency by the school.

This fund requires the school to make an application under the process outlined by the LA. This should be done as early as possible. The criteria and process should be published on the Schools Forum website.

Schools in Financial Difficulty Fund

Some LAs hold a fund for schools in financial difficulty. However, this has become rarer, as many Schools Forums are reluctant to reserve funding for this purpose when it could be spread across all schools. In a climate when many schools have to take difficult decisions, headteacher representatives are understandably wary of appearing to reward poor management of resources and will only support requests in unforeseeable or exceptional circumstances.

It is therefore increasingly unlikely that such a fund exists, but you should check with your Schools Forum representative. To be successful in an application, the school will usually need to prove that the difficulties have arisen as a result of extreme circumstances outside of its control.

DfE can provide funding to academies in financial difficulty, but it is not clear when a loan is provided and when a grant is awarded.

There is also an emergency funding source, the Strategic School Improvement Fund, for schools and academies subject to unexpected or imminent failure. Applications can be put forward by teaching schools, national support schools and multi-academy trusts, and in exceptional cases, individual schools may qualify. See https://www.gov.uk/guidance/strategic-school-improvement-fund-emergency-funding.

Funding and income

We advise you to take particular care not to mix up funding and income. Funding is provided by funding bodies such as LAs, DfE, ESFA, etc. Income is any payment that the school generates itself, such as donations or fees for services rendered.

However, this isn't an exact science, and some LAs may classify some types of funding as income, particularly those that vary during the year, such as SEND funding. It all depends on the local authority's individual accounting practices. So don't worry too much if some money is given as income in your area, but a school in a neighbouring authority receives it as a funding allocation.

The crucial thing is making sure you avoid double counting. Don't create an income line in the budget as well as including it in the total of available funding that you are balancing to. There's no quicker way of causing an overspend.

7 FINDING SOURCES OF INCOME

Where to start

If schools cannot rely on funding from the government to provide everything that they need, then finding other sources of funding to supplement it becomes essential. More and more schools are prioritising income generation as a safety net for survival. Watch out for our online course on Developing an Income Generation Strategy: https://schoolfinancialsuccess.com/online-courses-2/.

For schools that haven't tried to attract additional funding before, it can be daunting. But there is no reason school staff can't be entrepreneurs, thinking creatively about how to make the most of the school's assets. The key is to link it to the school's vision and get support from across the leadership team and Governing Board or Board of Trustees.

Think about the expertise that exists among your staff. Are there hidden talents, for example creativity that could be harnessed to make and sell items, expertise in marketing and use of social media, skills in IT or graphic design which you can sell to other schools, or experience in bid writing for a charity?

Assuming that you have the support of governors and SLT colleagues, you need to create a list of ideas that are worth exploring. A good starting point is identifying whether there is something that your community really needs which people would be prepared to pay for. A suggestion box may provide some excellent ideas from pupils, members of staff or governors.

Knowledge of what other schools are doing in your area can help, but be aware that someone else may have cornered the market in something, such as sports facilities or adult education classes. Don't forget to consider a joint approach with another school or a local organisation, where a combined effort might generate more benefit than each of you working independently.

You should develop a business plan for income generation, which must be based on the vision for the school. It has to be complementary to the priorities in the School Development Plan and must not represent a distraction. Taking a professional and methodical approach will prove you are serious about doing things differently. It will allow you to construct a set of ideas and think them through, identifying any investment that the school may need to make in order to kick start the plans. Risks can be identified and suggestions made for how they can be minimised or removed.

Barriers to income generation

Above all else, the culture in a school can form the biggest barrier to income generation. Some common excuses that you can be faced with when trying to persuade others to engage with entrepreneurial activity are:

- Lack of time
- Unsuitable premises
- No spare resources to devote to a project
- Insufficient experience and knowledge of how to do it
- Leadership team or governors won't support taking risks
- Concerns about safeguarding if others can use the school premises
- It will be a distraction from the core work of the school

Sometimes these objections are founded on nothing more than fear of change, but you can achieve anything if it is regarded as a priority. The key is to find ways of dealing with the main risks that others are afraid of.

Opportunities

Some of the opportunities open to schools can be categorised as follows:

- Applications for grant funded schemes
- Fund-raising by requesting donations
- Regular income generation through commercial enterprises and the provision of shared or traded services

Let's take a look at some examples of these.

Applications for grant funded schemes

There is a balance to be struck here. Some grant schemes involve time-consuming applications and/or very detailed monitoring and reporting requirements, some of which can cost far more in staff time to prepare than the benefit gained from the grant.

So, when considering whether to apply for new funding, think about the cost-benefit aspect. How much work will it take to prepare the application, and do you have someone with the necessary skills? If you already monitor the areas that they want to measure progress in, you have a ready-made baseline position and future reporting should not be onerous. Consider the amount of money on offer; is it worth the effort of applying?

Various providers offer grant finding services, a database of grants that are relevant to schools with up to date information provided by funding organisations. You should still check them out to make doubly sure that you qualify, otherwise you will waste your time preparing an application.

The key thing to remember is that funders want to give money for specific purposes, so there is little point in even applying if you don't match those. Be selective about who you approach and be clear about your own vision and how it fits with theirs, and you stand a much better chance of success.

Read all the information and provide everything they ask for. Give yourself plenty of time to prepare it; a late submission will probably go in the bin. Don't mess up your chances by ignoring the instructions!

Fund-raising

Fund-raising includes organising campaigns to generate donations from parents, local businesses and other interested parties, usually with a specific purpose in mind such as a large item of equipment or specialist facilities for extra-curricular activities relating to sports, arts or music.

A Parent Teacher Association can be worth its weight in gold. Parents and governors may have innovative ideas and lots of energy to carry them out. Let those running the PTA know what you need, which activities are acceptable and what support you can offer. Making sure they receive recognition for their efforts will also pay dividends.

The same would apply to an Alumni association; you may have a former pupil who is willing to go the extra mile for their old school. It is also worth asking your pupils to sound out family members in case they know anyone who is able to donate money or equipment. We've heard of businesses offering valuable equipment which the school could sell on.

In a secondary school, a challenge to form groups or year groups can work well, such as giving them each a small sum of money and running a competition to see who can get the biggest return from it. This can be linked to project based activities promoting initiative, creativity and leadership and often fits well as part of the PSHE curriculum. The possibilities are endless.

Commercial enterprises and traded services

This is possibly the main area where you may face objections, because it often involves allowing members of the community to use your school's assets, and it's important to safeguard them.

The best ideas are passive income projects, where you set something up which doesn't need much input to keep it going. One example could be solar panels. But remember to check what you are allowed to do with the building; if you are an LA school you will need permission, or if you are part of a multi-academy trust, the MAT may also need to give approval.

The most common enterprise is letting school facilities to community organisations. You don't have to do this yourself; you can employ a company to provide the service for commission. But you must get legal advice before signing any agreements and be sure that all safeguards are in place to protect pupils, staff, the building, equipment and so on.

Another avenue is to sell services to other schools. Outstanding teachers or middle leaders with specialist expertise can provide training at a daily rate, or help other schools to address an adverse inspection report. This can be a good retention strategy, giving excellent staff a new motivation and helping their professional development. You could also provide support services, for example if you have an IT expert with a talent for designing websites, or a good photographer who can produce brochures for other schools.

A particular risk applies to Trusts with charitable activities: they may have to pay tax on the profits from trading in areas outside of their primary purpose. However, if the turnover from this type of trading is below the small trading tax exemption limit, the Trust doesn't need to pay tax. This is therefore likely to be a concern for larger MATs or Foundation Trusts with a lot of LA maintained schools, rather than smaller Trusts.

As with all tax matters, this situation isn't straightforward, and the conditions can change, so it is best to check on the specific circumstances you are in. For more advice on this, you can refer to the gov.uk guidance page at: https://www.gov.uk/guidance/charities-and-trading.

These are only examples, but we hope they will be a springboard to generate other ideas. The important thing is to ensure that this activity fits with the school's core purpose and vision, and does not represent a distraction. You need to know what your school's 'risk appetite' is, and ensure that people, assets and money are all protected.

8 GATHERING INFORMATION FOR YOUR BUDGET

Be prepared

In Chapter 5, we looked at the budget cycle and advised you to start preparing early for the budget by gathering together all the information that you need. Being organised, with all the data to hand as you begin to put together your budget, makes it easier to spot any problems well in advance. But the benefits go further than this.

In a busy school, it can be hard to get a moment to think about a big task like budget preparation. Psychologically, it can be a little like the proverbial 'eating an elephant'. The advice is to take it one bite at a time.

The equivalent of this tactic in budgeting terms is to send out your requests for information early, then arrange meetings with relevant staff at appropriate times to discuss it. If you are using an incremental budgeting approach with some specific areas of focus, you will probably want to concentrate on any significant changes in activities that might result in a different level of spending. You may need to make extra provision in the budget for it, or there could even be a saving.

As you gather the information, your sub-conscious is likely to be working on it, storing away pertinent facts in your brain and thinking through any potential problems. Once you turn your attention to using the data and intelligence you have collected as the basis for your budget, you might experience a lightbulb moment, as a solution pops into your head for a particular problem that you've been grappling with.

The approach to information for budgeting

Information forms the basis of decision-making in a wide range of areas. You will already be familiar with the need for robust data on pupil assessment and test or examination results, as a foundation for ensuring educational success. Data and other information is crucial in identifying the support that pupils with particular difficulties need. Gathering information can make the difference between identifying what the real problems are and making inaccurate assumptions which might cause further difficulties for a child.

Information can be readily available within the school, but sometimes you need to consult other professionals from outside to find out the facts. This also applies to information needed for budget preparation and monitoring.

We will look at the different information that you need for the budget as we go through this chapter. But one crucial set of data is created annually in October and has already had an impact: the annual school census. This will govern the funding that you receive.

Whatever the type of information, here are four key principles that you need to pay attention to in order to achieve school financial success.

1. Accuracy

Accuracy is essential in every aspect of a school's activity. Decisions will be taken on the basis of data and information, and any inaccuracies could have serious consequences. Incorrect recording of pupil data could lead to the school receiving insufficient funding from the local funding formula.

Internally, pupil information will also be used as a basis for other decision-making which affects the budget: priorities for the school, future plans for expansion, school organisation for different patterns of admissions, and many other aspects related to the school's operations. Staffing details will be used in setting pay budgets, the most significant element of annual spending.

You also need to build the confidence of external stakeholders in your ability to provide information to them, such as the local authority and ESFA as your funding bodies. If they find your returns are inaccurate, it could have serious consequences, causing financial or reputational risks.

2. Timeliness

You need the most up to date information possible if you are to identify issues at an early stage and act on them. This could make the difference between a surplus and a deficit. If you realise early on that savings need to be made, you can develop a strategy that allows you to take advantage of staff turnover, which can help to avoid compulsory redundancies.

Timeliness is just as important as accuracy for decision-making. Senior leaders don't want to waste time working on old data, having to revise their analysis later when they realise more up to date information is available.

3. Robust data and financial systems

What should you expect from data and financial systems? They should be reliable, accurate and easy to use; complicated systems can lead to errors and confusion, which will pose a risk of poor decision-making. It should be possible for a system to flag up values that lie outside of tolerance levels, to improve the chances of errors being identified.

The ability to produce accurate and clear reports is crucial, particularly in the area of finance, which many people find daunting at the best of times. There is no benefit in having a lot of data in a system which you can't extract in a meaningful way. Within reason, people should be able to access the data according to their individual needs, with a robust audit trail to ensure that it is possible to trace any changes made. An audit trail is particularly important in relation to financial information.

All schools should ensure that they have appropriately skilled staff who can handle data, operate systems securely, and check data quality.

4. How to use, analyse and interpret data to get the best results

Different people will need different data for a range of purposes, and they will all have varying levels of competence and confidence. For example, governors will not want too much detail, as their role is strategic. Senior leaders responsible for budgets will want a high-level report but may also need to drill down to see a more detailed analysis of expenditure and income.

Your support staff need to be able to provide advice and guidance, without doing everything for managers. It is important to build confidence and provide training tailored to needs, so managers can develop skills and become competent enough to analyse the information themselves.

Having said that, sometimes it is quicker for data and finance staff to provide the information. It's a matter of judgement as to what constitutes the best use of everyone's time. When one member of staff is asking another for information, both have a responsibility to ensure a proper understanding of what the question is, i.e. what is really being asked for. Those who own the data may need to probe a little to make sure that any complications are understood, so that the information provided is fit for the intended purpose.

Analysing and interpreting data is a valuable skill; when faced with a range of options, hypotheses need to be formed and tested before taking decisions.

The key to all of this is giving yourself time to gather the information, and that means starting early enough. Let's now look at the type of information that you will find helpful to gather before starting to prepare the budget.

School Development Plan priorities

As already mentioned, it is essential to identify any activities and costs in your School Development Plan (SDP) which need to be incorporated in the budget. At this stage, you don't need to assess how you can afford them; if they are priorities, you will have to build them into the first draft of your budget. Once you have the full picture of your net expenditure compared to the available funding, then you can assess whether cutbacks may be needed elsewhere to allow these priorities to be funded.

We recommend that you check whether the costs built into the SDP are still valid and up to date. If you are a School Business Leader, you will usually have advised on the calculation of costs for the SDP, but there may have been changes in the delivery of activities or the costs since the SDP was written. Alternatively, another set of SATs or GCSE results may have been published by the time budget preparation is under way, meaning that some priorities and/or activities may have changed.

Be aware of the cycle for the SDP and budget, and try to blend them so that you are basing budget decisions on up to date priorities and activity costs. Refer back to the budget cycle in Chapter 5.

Seek clarification from those responsible for the activities, to find out how much flexibility there will be in the timescale. For example, will the activity require all the resources in the financial year you are budgeting for, or will expenditure be spread across financial years? This is particularly pertinent for LA schools where the academic year straddles two financial years. Have any balances been earmarked for the activities? If so, you will need to ensure that this element isn't committed for other things.

Pupil numbers, classes and school organisation

It is important to look at changes in your rolls for the year in question, as these can affect your need to spend. Will there be any reorganisation of classes that might impact on staffing and resources, including small groups for SEN or other additional needs? This is where the interface between the curriculum and staffing plans and the budget becomes important.

Do all year groups roll forward more or less unchanged, or does the school experience a lot of in-year turnover of pupils on roll, including international new arrivals? This can require extra resources to assess and work with new pupils to settle them in and find out what their abilities are. Knowing the general pattern of admissions may help you to consider the level of resources that may be needed in the budget.

If building work has taken place to enlarge the premises to accommodate extra pupils, you should try to obtain estimates of the increased consumption for energy and any impact on the level and cost of services such as cleaning and caretaking. Rates charges may change if the school changes in size, but you don't need to worry about this as the budget will normally be adjusted in-year by your funding body to match the actual expenditure.

Have you invested in significant amounts of new equipment, perhaps IT equipment or reprographics equipment which may have implications for increased energy consumption and future maintenance agreements?

Do you have all the information to hand for lease agreements or any other committed expenditure which spans more than one financial year, for example licences or subscriptions for digital resources or software packages?

Have you entered into any agreements for use of facilities in addition to your school building, perhaps for alternative education provision? What is your commitment and for what period?

Staffing information

Information on staff costs should be readily available through your HR system. You should also have to hand the Pay Policy and Appraisal Policy.

Key data include:

- Full time equivalent staff across all categories;
- Financial impact of term time only contracts, including any extra days paid over the year;
- Teacher contact ratios, directly impacting on teacher numbers;
- Known/planned changes for individual staff e.g. ending or beginning of temporary contracts, starters and leavers from normal turnover of staff including any gaps, maternity/paternity leave and changes in hours, all including any part-year effect;
- The cost of pay awards;
- Grade changes, whether through normal pay progression, performance management decisions or changes in responsibilities;
- National insurance and pension status of individual staff, which affect employer's contribution costs, and any changes in rates;
- Any planned changes in staffing due to curriculum changes or

restructuring, including leadership team changes;
- Changes in activities, e.g. traded services provided to other schools, or commercial ventures: what staff will be needed and at what cost?
- Estimates for overtime if this is a requirement for any particular teams, usually support staff. Examples could include caretaking for out of hours events or supporting the logistics of exam set-up during exam season for secondary schools.

Non-pay supporting information

The main categories of non-pay expenditure tend to be related to buildings, contracts for goods and services or consumables. The amount of information available depends on your local arrangements.

If you are part of large-scale procurement arrangements provided through local authorities or MATs, such as energy, broadband, or service level agreements for catering, caretaking, cleaning and grounds maintenance, then all you require is information on any proposed changes to specifications and price rises. If you have a Private Finance Initiative arrangement, price and service changes will be outlined within the original agreement and updates.

Where your school undertakes particular functions internally rather than by contracting with external organisations, you should already have taken into consideration any changes in staff costs. As well as inflation on consumables, you will need to know whether there are any changes planned in how the service is being carried out that might affect costs. You may sell the service to other schools, in which case knowing how costs will change will enable you to propose an appropriate set of charges.

Contract details should all be held in a contracts register; if any are approaching the end of their term, you should have plans in place for renewal, or be preparing for new quotations or tenders, depending on the costs.

Budget monitoring should highlight any areas that are proving difficult to control. Judgement is needed on whether an area is a genuinely volatile heading, or whether budget managers need more training to control it.

Income

The information needed for income budget preparation will depend on the sources relevant to your situation. For lettings, you should have a schedule of charges and agreements outlining the period of use, the expiry date and review periods. For other sources, you may need to gather information from previous years on the volume of activities and price levels.

Where ad-hoc bookings are part of your facilities hire arrangements, you will need to estimate a reasonable level of income based on a combination of previous year trends, changes to activities, price levels and any other factors that affect usage, including your customer base. Be aware of how school use of the facilities may be changing. If you require the space for school based activities and events outside of the school day, this may reduce the level of income you are able to generate.

See if there is any information available on the impact of previous price changes. There can be significant price resistance in relation to some activities, and if other schools or local organisations are offering similar facilities, you might have considerable competition.

Depending on your catering arrangements, you may receive paid meals income. Cross check this with any pupil number changes to see whether income might increase.

Refer to your income strategy (referred to in Chapter 7) to support your income budget preparation. Include only confirmed income or low-risk estimates which err on the side of caution. You may have a seemingly great idea for an income generation activity, but until you can see that idea develop into a reality it is a risk to include it in your budget and it could result in a deficit position if it is not successful.

Balances

Schools need to keep a working balance to allow for fluctuations in planned spending and emergencies. As mentioned in Chapter 5, each year's funding should support the pupils in school now, rather than stockpiling balances for some future event that may not occur. Saving up for a capital project is fine, as long as your current pupils are not deprived of resources.

The level of balances should be a deliberate strategy, not an accidental outcome. The preferred approach should be agreed with senior leaders and governors in a Reserves Policy. It should cover a multi-year period, taking into account trends in funding and rolls, allowing for any significant projects that need to be resourced and setting a target level of balances to aim for.

When the Audit Commission was in existence, the recommended levels of balances were 8% of budget share for primary and special schools, and 5% for secondary schools. These were only intended as guidance, but they are still sometimes used as a measure to identify schools with excessive balances.

We did have a period when the government encouraged LAs to claw back excessive balances and redistribute them across all schools, but that is no longer the case. Technically it is still possible, but usually schools will prove that they are holding them for a purpose to avoid this. There are different attitudes to this across the country, with some Schools Forum members exerting substantial pressure on their peers who hold high balances without specific plans for them, and others taking a much more relaxed attitude.

The policy should show the planned use of balances, which should be reviewed as each year's budget is being prepared. If there is any overspending during the year, prompt action will need to be taken to bring the overall budget back into balance, otherwise it could eat into the planned reserves, leaving insufficient money available for projects you have saved up for.

Estimating the balance to carry forward

If you are preparing the budget well in advance, you might not have a reliable prediction for the current financial year. However, you should have been calculating an estimated year end (outturn) position throughout the year and should therefore know the likely impact on the school's balances.

Be aware that there can sometimes be surprises quite late on in the year, due to funding adjustments outside of core allocations. We have already mentioned termly adjustments to nursery funding according to actual participation. The timing of these can vary in different LAs. Or there could be a revision of expenditure charged by the LA such as energy contracts.

You might experience a loss of income through bad debts from your customers, such as ad hoc lettings. The lesson here is to get payment in advance wherever possible. If that is impractical because it could affect custom, at least ensure you have their full details so you can chase payment.

You should examine the history of the school's balances over the last five years. Is there a pattern? Can you explain the changes from one year to the next or the general trend? Was it a planned trend or were there some unexpected results and what were the reasons for them?

An analysis of the last five years' final outturn statements at a detailed level will identify whether some budget holders regularly estimate that they will break even, but always have a surplus or an overspend at the year end. What is the profile of spending in the last few months of the year? Does anyone appear to have unusually high levels of expenditure in the last couple of months? This could suggest they spend up any remaining funding because they are afraid their budget will be permanently reduced if they underspend.

This sort of behaviour may represent a poor use of resources. If it is identified early enough, you can address it and free up money for cost pressures or new priorities in the SDP.

Identify any plans that are already in place for the use of balances, such as SDP priorities or contributions to capital projects which are suitable for one-off investment. You will need to ensure there is a basic contingency to cover any emergencies or unplanned overspending.

Local authorities and the ESFA are expected to monitor schools with excessive/rising surpluses and challenge them on their plans. Many still use the Audit Commission thresholds to identify these schools.

For academies, external auditors have to express an opinion as to whether they are a going concern or not. This is a question of whether the academy trust is able to meet its liabilities as they fall due. It's an issue that applies irrespective of whether or not the trust is expecting to be in deficit in the following year's budget; academies should be looking ahead over a three to five-year period and making sure that they can meet the requirement to show in their financial statements that the academy is a going concern. Trustees should not be relying on auditors to confirm this.

Another linked issue is the requirement outlined in the Academies Financial Handbook for academies to produce cash flow estimates. While funding is mostly allocated on an even monthly basis, expenditure doesn't follow the same pattern, and the timing of payments will need to be managed to ensure they don't exceed income in any given month. This will provide reassurance that income and expenditure is being managed in a way that guarantees a balanced budget.

Financial benchmarking

Whether you are anticipating problems in balancing your budget or not, eliminating waste will be a priority if you are to give learners the best chance of a good education. One way of achieving this is to compare your spending levels with similar schools using the DfE's financial benchmarking website: https://schools-financial-benchmarking.service.gov.uk.

The benchmarking site allows you to select a comparator group of schools or trusts with similar features, using criteria such as number on roll, age range, free school meal eligibility or proportion of pupils with SEND. It is important to select criteria carefully to find comparable schools/trusts. This can be tricky, as if you pick too many categories or use very narrow ranges, the tool may produce a group of schools that is too small to be of much use.

Ensure you analyse the information sensibly, highlighting areas which have high or low expenditure and income. Find out the real reasons you are appearing to spend at a higher level for some areas and remember to look across different groupings. For example, you may appear to have higher teaching costs per pupil than another school, but they may be organised differently and your classroom support staff costs per pupil may be lower.

The important thing is that you don't make excuses, but that you challenge yourself on why you have higher than average spending in some areas. DfE encourages schools to get in touch with their comparators if they identify some with lower expenditure and better attainment or progress. This is often not very straightforward, because the benchmarking data can quickly become dated, and there can be particular differences in the profile of a school which aren't obvious at first sight.

But don't let this put you off. Follow up any significant differences with comparator schools if they will share information with you. Most will be willing to discuss their experiences and you might be able to help them in some areas.

Your aim should be to identify areas for further investigation, signposting expenditure headings that might bear fruit in your search for efficiencies. This will help you make the best use of your time by focusing on the areas in which you are most likely to achieve gains.

9 STARTING TO PREPARE THE BUDGET

Involving staff

You will stand the best chance of keeping to a budget if staff throughout the school have had the opportunity to be involved in the process of preparing it. This could involve discussing the practical aspects of targeting spending to priorities, or generating ideas for making savings when it is proving difficult to balance the budget. Do you have a suggestion box? Often staff may be reluctant to make suggestions in a meeting or face to face with their manager, but will be willing to do it on an anonymous basis.

Staff involvement needs to be proportionate; a classroom teacher, teaching assistant or admin assistant will not have much interest in the details of the budget. But every member of staff is using up some of the resource, in the time they spend working or in the resources that they use. If they are aware of the importance of getting good value from the money allocated, they may think more carefully about what they do.

It is particularly important that middle and senior leaders have an awareness of the choices that have to be made in the budget. They have the potential to spend significant amounts of money on staff and resources, and if their decisions are at odds with the overall approach, you may find that you are not achieving value for the money that is spent. If you have very little spare funding left for contingencies once the budget is constructed, and budget holders do not realise this, any overspending could cause a deficit.

The difficulty is that finance is regarded with some nervousness by many people. Some find it hard enough to manage their own spending, let alone that of their organisation, and taking on responsibility for aspects of the school's budget can be scary. Some budget holders will take to it like a duck to water, but others will require considerable hand-holding and reassurance.

An approach which can help to build confidence in the overall budget is to have a transparent and documented system for allocating resources to budget holders. This should make clear how much is being allocated for ongoing commitments and for agreed developments. It will promote trust and make budget holders more willing to cooperate if they are asked to give up some budget to help with unexpected pressures.

So how do you engage staff in the budget process to achieve their cooperation and support, without it being too onerous? The table below offers some suggestions at different levels.

Who?	How?	What?
SLT	Bespoke training Regular updates Budget champions	• Sound understanding of the principles of value for money to support and be a role model for this culture • Regular updates through meetings on the whole school financial position, budget review process, income generation strategies and forward financial planning
Budget holders	Bespoke training	• Responsible for public money, make decisions and authorise spending • Sound understanding of the principles of value for money to support and be a role model for this culture • Transparency for how their budgets are allocated • Will be held to account throughout the year so must be suitably skilled
Finance staff	Bespoke training	• Detailed understanding of financial procedures and their role • Basic understanding of the bigger picture to enable them to challenge appropriately and contextualise their actions to the whole school budget process
All new staff during induction	Bespoke training	• Basic understanding of processes and procedures which may affect their role and level of responsibility • Sound understanding of the principles of value for money to support this culture
All staff	Financial bulletin/staff newsletter	• If your school is in a challenging position, regular communication to celebrate positive change and staff support could be a good tool to support staff buy-in.

Various tactics can be employed to promote cultural change, but the most effective are those that are highly visible. A workshop for staff, if handled well, can achieve innovative ideas, peer challenge and enthusiasm for change. You can identify champions (preferably willing volunteers) for particular areas of spending, with a remit to remind staff when they see waste and support them to change behaviours.

You can also involve pupils in age-appropriate ways, for example appealing to interests in conservation and eco-friendly approaches by asking them to research energy-saving measures that might work well in your school.

High level review

Once you have gathered together all the relevant information, you should undertake a high-level review of it. Ask yourself what the content tells you about the school's overall financial position. How secure is it? This is not a detailed exercise, but rather a broad-brush assessment to identify areas of vulnerability that could cause difficulties for your budget. It's better to be aware of potential issues that could trip you up before you encounter them.

Earlier, we mentioned the ability to read a budget as being an important skill that can tell you a lot about the way a school is operating. Here we look at some aspects of this ability, with a few tips on what to watch out for. None of this is difficult; it's a matter of being vigilant and analysing things logically.

Unless you are taking a zero based approach, your starting assumption for the new year's budget is that it will broadly follow a similar pattern to the current year, with adjustments for changes in activity and costs. Doing a high-level review should alert you to areas where changes are happening.

A good starting point is to assess the current year's outturn prediction as recently reported to governors, or an internal version if that is more up to date. If there are a lot of variances on individual lines in the report, this could be indicative of poor financial control, or a failure to update the budget to reflect changes in planned spending.

There is a risk that you might lose control of your money if you don't keep the budget dynamic by updating it to move money around to where it's needed. Budget holders who are underspending might assume they have their full budget available, whereas you might be planning to redirect those spare resources to offset an unexpected overspend in another area.

You should note any obvious areas where expenditure or income has historically tended to be out of line with the budget, and analyse the reasons for it. In some cases, you will need to make a judgement call on whether you should increase the amount allocated to such headings.

Particular caution is recommended when checking whether income targets have been achieved. Follow your instincts and ask for hard evidence if a budget holder insists they will achieve the target but it is getting late in the year and there is not much sign of money coming in. A debtor's invoice doesn't generate cash until it's paid by the customer. If the income budget is unrealistic, there will be a greater risk of overspending. This is an area where governors can make a challenge, asking what assumptions have been made about the level of income that is likely to be generated.

How does the financial benchmarking data look overall? Are there a lot of areas with high costs compared to similar schools, or a fairly even spread of higher and lower expenditure? Can you explain the most significant differences? Are your teaching and support staff budgets at a higher proportion of budget share than comparable schools, making you more vulnerable to cost pressures such as incremental drift, pay awards and changes in employer's national insurance and pension contributions?

You may not be able to do much about these issues in the short term, but being aware will help you to approach the rest of the budget with caution and consider the impact of these issues when taking staffing decisions in future.

Are your balances sufficient to cope with unplanned overspending? If you have a Licensed Deficit, is the recovery plan on track?

This high-level review should not take long, but it will give you a good indication of any weaknesses that might pose a risk to the school's financial sustainability. It will provide a check list of areas you need to pay particular attention to when preparing the budget. Don't forget to refer back to it as you go through the budget setting process.

You could incorporate these areas into a risk assessment table for discussion with SLT and the Governing Board, to get their views. This could result in agreement to move resources from other headings to cover any risks you have identified, or to allocate any additional funding that might become available, for example as a result of the National Funding Formula.

Budget structure

Before moving on to the actual preparation of the budget, it is worth considering how you will present it. There are two methods you can use:

- Financial accounting headings, used in statutory returns, i.e.

'subjective' expenditure headings: teaching staff, support staff, premises, supplies and services and transport.

- Management accounting categories, where you monitor spending on functions ('objective' headings), such as curriculum areas, SEND, nursery class or sixth form, leadership, pastoral support and so on.

The first of these is the format generally used in the finance reports submitted to your funding body, because the subjective headings form the basis of annual reporting by every school and academy in the country. It is aggregated upwards into national statistics on school spending, and feeds into the DfE's benchmarking websites for schools and academies.

You may wish to set up the second system as a separate version for management purposes if that is more meaningful. It will entail extra time and effort, because you must make sure you reconcile the two and you still need to use the national format for statutory submissions. Every item of expenditure and income must be included in your reports, forming the basis for good decision-making.

Risk management

A contingency budget should be set to cover known risks in constructing your budget, especially but not exclusively in pay headings. Let's consider a few examples of the risks.

Performance pay makes it harder to predict salary progression. No longer can you assume most teachers will work their way through the main scale one rung at a time. Some may receive increases equating to more than one move up the pay range. The school's Pay Policy should define the terms 'highly competent', 'substantial' and 'sustained', to substantiate decisions.

Of course, teachers who are performing well should be credited with a pay award that reflects their performance. Reducing budgets and other cost pressures are not a justification for not recommending or approving a pay award for an individual.

If the Pay Policy defines 'sustained' as a two-year period and a member of staff was awarded a double pay award in the previous year, then they shouldn't be eligible for another 'double' pay award until two years later.

To establish a meaningful amount for the contingency budget, every member of teaching staff will need to be considered, with some discussion amongst key senior leaders as to what is possible and what is likely. The contingency budget will be based on professional judgement and is not an exact science, but does ensure there is some resource allocated should eligible teachers be awarded such pay progression.

Another risk is teacher recruitment difficulties, which may lead to the offer of incentive payments, or 'golden handcuffs' for retention of outstanding teachers. It is vital that you build these into your budget.

If you have a nursery, are you offering the extended 30-hour nursery entitlement? Consider the potential take up carefully; it can be difficult to judge demand and the funding may not fully cover the costs.

You also need to be watchful for changes in legislation and other developments which affect levels of expenditure. For example, increases in employers' national insurance and pension contributions are likely to occur in the Chancellor's Budget Statement or whenever a review of pension schemes is conducted. It's also possible for entirely new commitments to be created without funding, such as the Apprenticeship Levy for some schools.

After a long period of speculation and anxiety, the employer's contribution for the Teachers' Pension Scheme was increased significantly in September 2019, from 16.48% to 23.68% of contributory pay. While a grant was offered and is being transferred into core funding, there could be further pressures, because the higher rate naturally applies to future pay increases and changes to the pay structure such as the uplift for early career teachers.

10 PAY BUDGETS

Budgeting for teaching staff

This chapter provides a framework for developing pay budgets, the most significant part of your resourcing plans. The first section examines the process for building teacher pay budgets for a one-year plan. We will then go on to look at support staff budgets.

We have already mentioned the need for strong links between the curriculum, staffing and school development plans and the budget. Here is where you will be putting these links into practice. Your pay budget should reflect the staffing plan, which considers the number of teachers available and their specialist and non-specific knowledge and skills. This plan is informed by the curriculum plan that determines what staff will deliver.

There are many different strands to budgeting for teaching staff, including the allocation of staff to subjects, leadership and management duties, class sizes, teacher contact ratios, allowing for PPA time, and the staffing needed for small groups or specific support for pupils at risk of under-achieving. These elements can make a significant difference to the teacher pay budget requirement. The DfE recommends Integrated Curriculum-Led Financial Planning (ICFP) as a tool for balancing the different elements. This approach aims to achieve the desired curriculum in the most efficient way. Various organisations have designed their own versions of ICFP.

Considering these issues afresh can sometimes lead to a realisation that some teachers are not being used at maximum effectiveness or efficiency. Are some of them tied up in routine or administrative tasks that could be done by a member of the support staff?

One particularly complex aspect is the need to estimate where your teaching staff will be within the pay ranges when setting your budget. Here we offer some thoughts about how to make a reasonable set of forecasts.

Pay structure and forecasting for teachers

Regardless of your school type or phase, it is not as easy as it used to be to forecast teacher pay budgets. Before the introduction of performance related pay, teachers were paid on a set national scale, with defined points and incremental movement through the scales relating directly to the number of years in the profession. The only real variations to this were London and Fringe payments. This made for a straightforward forecasting exercise when it came to budget setting for future years.

However, everything changed when performance related pay came along. The move away from a 'one size fits all' approach to a more tailored approach to suit individual schools has added an unprecedented layer of complexity to the biggest area of school spend.

Forecasting across multiple financial years for the same group of teaching staff could now have many possible outcomes. At one extreme, none of the staff in this hypothetical group might make any salary progression if their performance does not warrant it. Apart from any cost of living pay awards, their financial remuneration may not change at all. At the other extreme, they may all be awarded salary progression based on performance for all five years and in the case of 'highly competent' teachers making a 'substantial' and 'sustained' contribution to the school, this could result in a higher salary jump equivalent to more than one old style point on the pay range.

With the weightings being applied in the pay structure to get NQTs to a higher starting salary, the cost of the pay award to your school will also vary according to the mix of experienced and newer entrants to the profession.

So how can school leaders plan effectively into the future when there is so much uncertainty? Before schools can begin to make a meaningful financial forecast of teachers' pay, the systems and policy set-up in the school must be in place, compliant with national guidelines and regulations. It must also meet the requirements of the school and the individuals within it.

Six key areas for pay budgeting

We've identified six key areas within an annual pay budget approach:

1. Planning cycle
2. Policy
3. SMART appraisal objectives
4. Appraisee, appraiser and governor understanding
5. Roles, responsibilities and pay recommendations
6. 'Pay without points'

Let's see how these can form a robust process for setting pay budgets.

1. Planning cycle

For maintained schools and academies, budget setting occurs before the outcome of the annual pay review is known (by the end of October). As teacher pay progression is usually backdated to 1 September each year; this will mean a full year cost for an academy (year-end 31 August) and seven-twelfths of the financial year for a maintained school (year-end 31 March).

This makes even a one year budget a bit of a guessing game. For multi-year budgets, there is even more reliance on estimations and assumptions. Everyone involved in financial management in the school should know and understand this cycle and the implications it has for accuracy in financial forecasting. You will need to check your pay budgets as soon as the outcomes from the pay review are known, and transfer money from a general contingency if costs are higher than your original forecast.

2. Policy

There are two key school policies which are critical in this area; the Pay Policy and the Appraisal Policy.

<u>Pay Policy</u>

The Pay Policy should ensure that all employees are treated fairly and consistently in relation to pay and pay related issues. It should adhere to:

- The current School Teachers' Pay and Conditions document;
- Conditions of Service for School Teachers in England and Wales (Burgundy book);
- The National Joint Council for Local Government Services National Agreement of Pay and Conditions (Green book);
- The School Staffing (England) Regulations 2009 (as amended); and
- The Education (School Teachers' Appraisal) (England) Regulations 2012

One of the aims of the Pay Policy should be to ensure that the school manages its salaries and staffing costs within overall budget limits. The lower and upper limits of any pay ranges should be stated, along with any notional 'points' on the pay range if used. All relevant pay ranges should be included:

- Main (MPR)
- Upper (UPR)
- Leadership (LPR)
- Unqualified teacher (UQTPR)

Criteria for Teaching and Learning Responsibility (TLR) points and SEN allowances also need to be set out.

The Pay Policy should define the terms 'highly competent', 'substantial' and 'sustained', as individuals must prove they meet these criteria to qualify for a higher than usual pay award, sometimes referred to as a double jump. These should be exceptional cases rather than the norm, where the member of staff proves themselves to be highly competent, makes a substantial overall contribution to the school and sustains it over a period clearly defined in the Pay Policy. A sustained period in this context is usually more than one year.

Appraisal Policy

The Appraisal Policy sets out the framework for a clear and consistent assessment of overall performance of teachers and the headteacher. It is the appraisal process which informs any pay recommendations made to the appropriate layer of governance for approval.

LA schools are likely to tailor and then adopt the LA Pay Policy and Appraisal Policy. Academies will develop their own polices. While academies have greater freedoms in pay, in both cases the fundamental principles and policy aims should be the same. Importantly, these policies should go through a process of consultation with unions, be approved by the appropriate governance accountability layer and be shared with school staff.

It is critical that both the Pay Policy and Appraisal Policy are in place and meet all requirements, as they should ensure a robust evidence base for pay decisions and are fundamental building blocks of school financial success.

3. SMART appraisal objectives

Within the Appraisal Policy it should be recognised that appraisal objectives should be SMART (Specific, Measurable, Achievable, Realistic and Time-bound). These elements are important to ensure fairness and consistency for all staff. Objectives should also be appropriate to the appraisee's role, responsibility and level of experience.

If this is not the case, there could be an enhanced risk of challenges to the decisions made. This would create uncertainty for the budget.

4. Appraisee, appraiser and governor understanding

At the time objectives are set, appraisees and appraisers must fully understand what they are agreeing. They must be able to assess progress towards these throughout the year and measure success at the end of the appraisal cycle. If objectives are clear and progress is appropriately monitored, there should be no surprises for the staff member when the pay recommendation and pay decision is made.

A lack of understanding in the early stages can lead to confusion and a lack of clarity later in the process. This could lead to a member of staff appealing against a decision not to approve a pay award, if they believe they have successfully achieved what they understood to be asked of them. Communications must be in place to inform the person preparing the budget of any decisions that are overturned if it has an implication on the pay budget.

Governor understanding of objectives is also critical, to ensure they can make an accurate professional judgement that the evidence provided proves an individual has successfully met their objectives or otherwise.

5. Roles, responsibilities and pay recommendations

It is also important to ensure that everyone involved in the process understands their role and their level of responsibility. For example, it is the role of the appraiser to recommend pay progression where they feel that objectives have been met. It is then the role of the Headteacher to quality assure and moderate the process and make final recommendations to the appropriate layer of governance for approval. Only following governor approval should the member of staff then be informed of any pay progression or otherwise. Any movement would be backdated to 1st September and must be taken into account in the budget.

The governor role is two-fold. Firstly, a delegated Committee, usually the Finance Committee, will 'approve' or 'not approve' recommendations made by the Headteacher for every individual member of staff. Secondly, a selected panel of governors will hear individual staff appeals against any pay decisions.

6. 'Pay without points'

The national teachers' pay scales used to have defined points on which schools had to pay teachers. This applied to all the different scales in use with the two most commonly used scales for qualified teachers looking like this:

Main Pay Scale: MPS1, MPS2, MPS3, MPS4, MPS5, MPS6

Upper Pay Scale: UPS 1, UPS2, UPS3

These scales are now referred to as pay ranges, with a lower and upper limit in which schools can pay teaching staff anywhere they choose, within the freedoms of their Pay Policy and appropriate to the teacher's performance, based on competence and overall contribution to the school.

For budgeting purposes, it is obviously much easier to make forecasts when points on a scale are clearly defined and there is a set path which teachers' pay follows over a known period. Many schools continue to adopt notional 'points' within the pay ranges to create clarity for teachers, school leaders and governors. This allows the person setting the annual and medium-term budget plans to predict costs using meaningful assumptions.

With more fluid pay arrangements, predicting future costs can be very difficult. One way around this may be to include in the Pay Policy what a 'one point equivalent' move up the pay range would look like in monetary terms. So, for example, there could be a recommendation of £1,000 for good performance and perhaps £2,000 for highly competent performance and substantial contribution to the school evidenced over a sustained period. Remember that defining what the terms 'highly competent', 'substantial' and 'sustained' mean in this context is crucial in the Pay Policy.

It is manageable to have a have a small percentage of staff on random or ad-hoc 'points' within the pay range, but if a school has a large teaching staff all paid at different amounts within the pay range, this can quickly become unmanageable and make meaningful financial forecasting extremely difficult, not to mention extra work in updating payroll details and increasing the scope for errors. This can have a detrimental impact on the efficient and effective use of resources and future financial viability of the school. Schools which recognise this situation could consider how they might change their Pay Policy and implement a plan to resolve this issue over time.

Budgeting for staff other than teachers

Budgeting for staff who are not on teaching terms and conditions tends to be a much easier exercise than for teachers, if your structure for the coming year is known and staff are in post. The NJC scales consist of grades with a maximum of three incremental points in each grade. Staff automatically move through the points within a grade in April each year until they reach the top of the grade. They can only progress to the next grade if they are promoted due to an increase in level of responsibility, i.e. a different role.

If you are a community school with staff employed by the local authority, you will need to observe the local single status arrangements to ensure that equal pay legislation is complied with. A member of staff can bring a case if they are being paid a different grade compared to someone in another community school doing the same job. If the LA has given advice that the grade must be changed and the school has not followed this advice, the school is likely to be required to pay the costs of any court action as well as compensation payments. For all other types of school, whether Voluntary Aided, Foundation Trust or academy, the comparator staff are only those within the same employer group.

If you do not have any plans for internal promotion or movement of staff into new roles following a staffing review, the financial forecasting software you use to predict salaries will calculate support staff salaries for the coming year accurately and you be confident that your estimates are reasonable.

If you are planning a structure review, or movement of staff between roles, this exercise may be a little more complex but will still result in a reasonably accurate salary forecast. If there is the potential to adopt one of a number of scenarios, your financial forecasting software will support scenario planning and will help you make an informed decision about which scenario best meets the school's needs and supports your school's financial health.

Allowances for support staff can also be easily managed and predicted through the use of financial forecasting software and should not pose too much of a problem for budget predictions.

For staff other than teachers, who are paid on any scale other than the NJC scales, the same principles can be applied, as other scales also do not usually bring the same complexities and challenges as performance related pay on the teaching scales.

Non-contract pay costs

It is important to consider other pay costs which do not directly link to staff contracts. For example, your support staff may be the most likely to incur overtime. To ensure value for money, you should have procedures in place to ensure staff only work overtime with the prior agreement of their line manager, approved by the budget holder if this is somebody different.

For the purposes of forecasting costs for the budget, it is a good idea to start by looking at previous year trends, then use your knowledge of the school context and specific issues that may impact on the need for overtime. For example, if you are planning a one-off building project that will involve site staff outside of their normal contracted hours, has this been factored in?

Also consider casual staff costs which will not be included in your staffing forecasts based on contracts of employment. Supply staff, exam invigilators and casual staff to support an evening and weekend community programme are budget areas where you will take a different approach to forecasting.

Look at previous year trends and use any other information available which may suggest variations from historic patterns. Remember to account for any on-costs such as employer's tax and national insurance contributions. Consider the entitlement to holiday pay for casual staff, which can make a significant difference to the cost of these staff.

Systems to support pay budgeting

Financial forecasting software has come a long way over the last decade. Gone are the days of building complex spreadsheets; most schools already use software for this purpose, which can be used for the forthcoming annual budget as well as for the medium term. Once the baseline year is correct, it will roll forward for future years, so you only have to tweak it for leavers, new starters, contract changes and movement in or out of pension schemes.

Pay awards are usually easily incorporated with these systems, although the government does not always announce its decisions early enough for schools to make a reliable assessment of the impact on their budgets.

You may be using an HR module linked to the finance module in a standard MIS package. For those who aren't, or are looking for something better, there are several packages available that can save school leaders hours of work, producing far more accurate results than most of us could concoct ourselves. There is inevitably a cost to these software packages, but shop wisely and the benefit of your investment will outweigh any costs.

A good financial forecasting package should be easy to use with appropriate training. The reporting element is very important. Reports should be easy for finance practitioners to interpret and present to other stakeholders who may have less financial experience. Some packages also link budget forecasting to school development planning which many find useful.

Prudence

Even with budget planning software, schools still need to make certain assumptions to ensure that their financial forecasts are as meaningful and accurate as possible. Most software packages allow salaries to be 'auto-incremented' in line with the background settings which the user usually has an element of control over. It is critical that background settings and individual salary increments are checked, double checked and triple checked to ensure that the overall salary forecasts align with the school's policy and any other known information.

In line with the accounting principle of prudence, expenditure must not be understated. For this reason, the aim is to create a worst-case scenario (financially speaking) of the salary costs. This also needs to be a realistic judgement. It is unlikely that every teacher in the school will be awarded an annual pay progression of more than one move up the pay range, so that doesn't seem a sensible assumption.

It would, however, be good practice to assume that every teacher will progress the equivalent of one move up their appropriate pay range. If some teachers don't, this will produce an underspend on the teacher pay budget, which can be reallocated to meet other needs in the school. If you are having problems in setting your budget, you should review the actual results of pay progression as soon as they are available, and adjust the budget accordingly.

This approach is based on a school's staffing structure remaining the same. If it is known that a role may change, resulting in a greater pay award, then this must be also be taken into account in financial forecasting.

Forecasting pay budgets can be a complicated task, but spending time getting this right is essential for a budget to be viable and achievable. Projecting non-pay budgets can also be complex but brings a different set of challenges, as we discuss in the next chapter.

11 NON-PAY BUDGETS

Non-pay value for money

The non-pay elements of a school budget comprise a wide range of activities, so you can't take a blanket approach to them. One of the challenges is that more people are able to influence spending across these headings, and therefore establishing a value for money culture can be quite tricky.

What do we mean by establishing a value for money culture? It is mainly about behavioural patterns and the way of life within the organisation. What is the culture in your school? Are staff and pupils always financially aware and efficient, or do they sometimes use resources without thinking, resulting in little or no positive impact?

When funding isn't an issue, it is easy for the financial culture to become more lax than we would like. Resources are taken for granted if they are available in abundance. Paper is wasted, forty one-sided colour copies are printed (just in case) instead of thirty black and white double sided, and an external minibus is hired when the school minibus is in use, even though your activity could have moved to another day; the list goes on.

It is not a case of staff deliberately being inefficient. When you are under pressure, you take the easiest path and that is often the one that doesn't involve thinking too hard about doing things differently. We all have habits that we fall into without challenging ourselves on why we do it like that. Without an impetus to change, we simply don't see the need to alter our ways.

The school funding reforms and ongoing cost increases will certainly provide that impetus for many schools. What is needed is strong financial leadership to prompt the organisation and individual staff to start to think differently and change their behaviour.

Here's a quick guide to how to achieve this in a positive manner and avoid instilling despondency or panic.

Be honest:

- about the funding situation and the challenges faced
- about the cost of waste and what it is equivalent to
- demonstrate the equivalent high value resources the school could have instead for the same value, e.g. staff member, IT devices, additional building capacity.

Remind people:

- that the school's money is public money and staff are accountable and have a professional responsibility for how it is spent.

Educate pupils:

- set a good example to them
- prepare them for the world of work, when they too will be expected to operate within a financially efficient culture.

Be a role model:

- senior leaders and governors should be role models for all staff, setting an example in cultural behaviours
- this starts with reviewing your own behaviours and changing where you need to
- as well as individual behaviours, have you thought about how all areas of the school are managed? This is a direct reflection of the senior leadership team. Can you be confident that the systems you have in place promote a positive financial culture? Staff may feel discouraged to make small changes to their own behaviour if they don't feel that the bigger issues are being tackled.
- all staff should be role models to pupils and other stakeholders - this is our school and this is how we work here, because this is how we get the best for everyone. Pupils may be good allies, especially in promoting the environmental impact of wasted resources, or providing a user perspective on how certain activities are organised.

You can identify champions (preferably willing volunteers) for particular areas of spending, with a remit to remind staff when they see waste and support them to change behaviours.

Examples of common cultural financial inefficiencies in schools include:

a. Use of supply cover
b. Printing/reprographics costs
c. External vehicle hire

d. Stationery and other general resources
e. Catering for meetings and events
f. Multiple delegates attending conferences outside of the local area

Identify these or any other areas of the budget where your costs are high, remembering to consult the results of your benchmarking exercise. Ask yourself why? Is it justified? If not, what can you change?

Cultural change starts with leaders and relies heavily on consistent and continued role modelling of behaviours. There must be buy-in at all levels for cultural change to take effect and it does not happen overnight. When it does start to take effect, financial leadership should remain focused and forward looking, to prevent a cultural slip back to old ways.

This sort of change is not easy to achieve, but is an investment of time and effort that pays you back. When faced with funding challenges, the alternative of doing nothing is not an option.

Practical budgeting tips

Here we explore some of the more common non-pay budget headings and suggest some approaches to help you develop a robust and reliable estimate of costs for the coming year. Your own circumstances and priorities may be different, but we hope these tips on what sort of issues to watch out for will be useful and that you can apply them across the board.

Staff development costs

Allocation of funding to Professional Development (PD) of staff should be based on a systematic approach. It should reflect national priorities, the school's priorities for development and the individual professional needs of individual staff identified through appraisal. By targeting your staff development budget appropriately, it will not only be more effective in the impact on teaching and learning; it will provide better value for money and the spending should be more controllable.

Evaluation of courses attended in the past should tell you which are a good use of staff time, or which need a different provider or an in-house approach. Attendance at an external course is not the only way of achieving PD; internal mentoring, coaching or delivery of material in either group sessions, drop-in sessions or online modules are all examples of other approaches that can be cost effective and have just as much impact, if not more. When staff feel that they have a choice about their professional development, with a rich and appropriate menu to choose from, they tend to be more motivated towards the training and gain more from it.

When assessing the most appropriate format for staff development, you should consider the full cost. How will the member of staff's absence be covered, if required? A day at a course in another part of the country will involve travel, the cost of the course, possibly some subsistence, and potentially supply cover. In contrast, an online course or mentoring within the school can be done in non-contact time.

If staff attend external training, consider how their learning can be disseminated in school to maximise efficiency. Can presentations and notes be shared with colleagues in a dedicated network space for example? It may be appropriate for the member of staff to deliver training to colleagues on their return, as part of the professional development calendar.

As with any school spending, the most important part of the evaluation process is to assess the impact the training has had on pupil outcomes. Avoid repeating training that has not proved any positive impact and even if it has, remember to assess if the needs of the pupils and the school are still the same. Curriculum changes, such as GCSE reform, may mean that a whole new approach is required.

Premises costs

Energy and some other premises costs can be difficult to predict, especially if you have made alterations to your buildings to accommodate more pupils or provide special facilities for those facing particular barriers to learning such as English as an Additional Language, disadvantage or SEND.

You may be able to work with experts during the process of any building alterations work, ideally at the design stage, to make some broad-brush estimates of the future operational running costs, particularly if you are adding a new building or block. Remember though, even with a plethora of technical information and assumptions these are just estimates and close monitoring of these budgets in the first year is essential. Even with expert help, this is still a very difficult task, as no-one can accurately predict levels of activity and usage. You will have to work on best guesses until you have a pattern of actual charges and trends to inform future forecasts.

For existing buildings, energy estimates can be more accurate but are still very difficult to predict. Obtain as much information as you can from energy companies, or your LA/Foundation Trust/MAT if you are part of a larger contract, to try to understand future price changes and how these will affect your bills. Always be aware of how your method of payment can support best value. Will you be charged extra for late payment, or even worse, be cut off? Would you get a discount for using direct debit? Pay particular attention to your procedures for paying invoices on time during holiday periods.

Your funding body will usually advise you of the amount to include in your budget for building rates. This is generally a 'budget neutral' item, meaning that if the actual rates charged are different to the estimate, your funding will be adjusted to match the cost. But do check with your funding body in case they are an exception to the rule. If you have recently become a Foundation Trust school or an academy, you will pay a lower level of rates, because charitable status usually qualifies you for rate relief. This does not mean you will achieve a saving; your funding will also reduce.

Repairs and maintenance is another difficult area to predict, as it is responsive, unlike planned maintenance. Analysing budget and expenditure trends from previous years may help to inform forecasting decisions for Repairs and Maintenance. Is there a particular type of damage that your school is prone to, such as vandalism or damage from adverse weather?

Have you delayed repairs to equipment and now realise it needs to happen in the year you are planning for? Involving staff in the discussions is a useful approach to ensure you have as much information as possible about the state of buildings and equipment. It may bring things to your attention that you were not aware of.

It is essential that you have an appropriate level of buildings and equipment maintenance plans in place to ensure health and safety, keep your facilities operational and reduce the need for emergency repair, which can bring about higher costs.

Ensure all buildings and contents are insured appropriately and check the detail of the policy carefully. When renewing, pay particular attention to the specification, to make sure you have the right level of cover.

Always try to build in a contingency to respond to unpredictable items.

Supplies & Services

Be aware of the impact of pupil numbers on this area of expenditure. Changes in the number, size and organisation of classes could affect your spending, or new specialist provision or small groups may have been set up.

Your school may provide certain services in-house, in which case you will have allowed for staffing in your pay budgets, but there could also be an implication for your non-pay budgets such as consumables. Be watchful for any changes between in-house and procured services (in either direction) and make any necessary adjustments to budget lines.

Contracts for goods and services can be a significant element, particularly catering, cleaning and caretaking. Having a clear specification for services will avoid any misunderstandings and ensure that the contract delivers what you need. Make sure the budget reflects any changes to specifications and/or renegotiated contracts as well as price increases.

Larger groups of schools and MATs procuring contracts for significant activity levels, such as school catering, will need to watch out for EU procurement rules. The implications of not following these can be serious. If the cost of the contract(s) goes above the threshold, you will need to observe these rules carefully; they can significantly extend the period for tendering. As these processes are intended to achieve value for money and a transparent process, it seems likely that even after Brexit there will be a similar set of requirements.

You can find out more about the principles and current requirements at the following DfE guidance page on Buying for Schools:
https://www.gov.uk/guidance/buying-for-schools.

The Buying Strategy also contains a host of links to different tips and tools at https://www.gov.uk/government/publications/schools-buying-strategy.

Where the contract includes performance indicators, have any penalties been incurred by the provider for not achieving them? This will generate a one-off saving; if you know about a retrospective refund, you will be able to incorporate it in your budget, but remember to remove it in the following year. A better approach might be to include it in your contingency.

If you are a local authority school, you may be accessing commissioning and procurement support. If you are part of a Multi-Academy Trust, there may be a central point in the Trust that deals with contracts. Use them for information, advice and guidance on issues to consider in your budget.

For smaller items, having internal controls goes a long way to minimising waste. You need to check that staff are not purchasing things individually, without any assessment of whether they are achieving value for money. By gathering together all your requirements and placing bulk or recurring orders, it will be possible to negotiate discounts for higher volumes or regular orders, which will also bring benefits to your budget.

If your school is collaborating with other schools for shared services, a lead school or MAT will make a charge for their time, but this should be reasonable in relation to the work done. Don't forget to take this into account in the budget.

Where appropriate, keep a renewal calendar for any annual services you buy. Carry out an annual review to decide if the service is still necessary and still represents value for money, allowing enough time to give notice to terminate the agreement. Otherwise, you may be obliged to continue with a service you don't really need. It is also useful to contact service providers to discuss renewal early, if you do want to continue. There are often savings to be made from signing up early. With more time to negotiate prices, you are in a much better position to get the best deal for your school.

Income

We have already mentioned that an important issue to watch out for is whether you are being over-ambitious about income targets. If you charge for training, or rent out your premises to community groups, make sure your budget is realistic and achievable. An income budget that is not achieved will result in an overspend.

It is usually better to under-estimate, but this can be a delicate balancing act if you have a very difficult budget; the last thing you want to do is make a member of staff redundant unnecessarily. Gather as much information as you can to establish what a realistic income target would be.

The income budget needs to reflect the activities the school is engaged in. Some are easier to estimate than others - e.g. regular rental income. Others may be sporadic and inconsistent, such as donations from local businesses or fund-raising by the Parents and Friends Association. Be prudent and you will avoid any nasty shocks during the year when income doesn't materialise.

12 FINALISING THE BUDGET

Balancing the budget

Once you have made a first pass-through of your budget, checking that all relevant activities and costs have been included, the next step is to total all expenditure and deduct income to identify the net expenditure. Compare the result with the available funding, but remember to separate funding from income, checking you haven't double counted any of it.

Ensure you have included all types of funding in your target total, referring to our chapter on available funding. Check you have included any reserves or deficit brought forward from the previous financial year.

If you are part of a MAT, the Trust may have set reserve targets for all its academies, to ensure the Trust as a whole is financially sustainable. Otherwise, you should know your own target from your reserves policy approved by governors, which forms part of your overall financial strategy.

When considering the target level of reserves, strong financial management is a key focus for all schools and academies. This needs to reflect your resource requirements to cover any known issues such as falling rolls, changes in staffing, improvement priorities, and any revenue contribution to capital costs for developments such as expansion or refurbishment. You will want to keep a reasonable general contingency for unforeseen events.

But as we have already mentioned, academies also need to ensure that they have sufficient reserves as a cushion to help avoid cash flow difficulties. This is a key performance indicator and needs to be considered as a priority.

Do you have a surplus, or a shortfall? Now is the time to double check the estimates against the previous year's actual spending and income, allowing for known changes in activities. Make sure they are realistic, reflecting the true cost of running the school in line with the vision and SDP. You should be able to explain the reasons for significant movements since the previous year's budget. Keep a record of the change and the reasons for it.

In chapter 8 we looked at a Reserves Policy, ensuring that you have a target to aim at when compiling the budget each year. How close are you to your target level of reserves after allocating money to all the budget headings? Is it close enough to need only a few tweaks to some budgets? Or is a more fundamental budget review needed? If so, our companion book 'Leading a School Budget Review' will provide a comprehensive set of guidance.

Surpluses

If there is a large surplus, check that you haven't missed any budget lines or elements within large cost centres. It's surprising how easily this can be done. Be aware of any substantial increase in funding. If you can't attribute it all to rising rolls or changes to the funding formula, there could be an error.

Check whether there are any significant changes in activity that haven't been reflected in expenditure. If rolls are rising, have you fully reflected the extra costs for staffing and resources? Remember there is a delay in funding for additional pupils. If you need new classes in September, check if you are entitled to any allocations from a Growth Fund, if the LA holds one.

Otherwise, for lower levels of growth which do not meet basic need requirements (i.e. don't fulfil the LA's need for school places), you will have to absorb the extra costs until the next financial year. The higher rolls will only be funded from the following April for LA schools, and the following September for academies, unless your GAG funding is based on estimates.

If you receive additional funding as a result of changes to the local funding formula, think carefully about how you are going to use it. Are there some important priorities that need to be funded? If performance is not as strong as it should be, any surplus should be invested in effective strategies to address under-performing groups of pupils.

In the current climate of uncertainty, it is tempting to build up balances as a cushion. But bear in mind what we have already said about the undesirability of accumulating excessive balances and depriving those children who are currently in your school of their entitlement.

Deficits

If you have a shortfall in the budget once you have completed it, the next steps depend on whether you have a cumulative surplus to bring forward.

In the year ended 31st March 2019, over 40% of LA schools spent more than their annual funding, either dipping into reserves, falling into deficit or increasing an existing deficit. We can't make a valid comparison with individual academy balances, as they are only published at trust level, but surveys suggest a similar situation. Unless your balances are very high, you can only go on depleting them for so long before facing a real risk of a deficit.

The percentage of LA schools with a cumulative deficit at March 2019 was 8% in primary, 28% in secondary and 13% in the special school sector. While the average percentage of trusts in deficit was lower, that doesn't include academies in deficit whose trust is in surplus overall.

In Chapter 5, we explain the process for schools and academies in deficit. Running a deficit is to be avoided if at all possible; as well as having a detrimental impact on morale in the school, it makes it even more difficult to handle unfunded cost pressures and emergency spending. So it's vital that you alert your funding body as soon as you become aware that it will not be possible to balance the budget.

Early awareness and action is also essential because it can take a long time to achieve savings, especially in pay budgets where you need to incorporate consultation and notice periods if compulsory redundancies have to be pursued. If you are an LA school starting the process in April, it will obviously not be possible to achieve a full financial year's savings. You may have to cut more posts or resources than if you had started earlier.

The same is true for changes to contracts. Unless there is a convenient break clause, you could be tied into a contract for a long period. Occasionally it may be worth paying a fee to extricate the school from it, but only if the overall impact of the change over the original contract period is a net saving. You also need to build in plenty of preparation time if you are tendering for a new service or provision of goods in order to save money.

Recovery plan

The LA and ESFA will require a school or academy trust that falls into deficit to develop a recovery plan to bring the budget back into balance within a period of up to three years. This plan needs to be robust and achievable, reflecting the school or trust's priorities so that standards are not put at risk.

Representatives from the funding body should keep in touch at regular intervals to discuss the progress made with the recovery plan, and to challenge you if it is not on track to balance at the end of the agreed period.

Our book 'Leading a School Budget Review' will be invaluable in guiding you through the steps to take if you are in this situation. Prompt action is needed to kick start the process of getting the budget back on track.

Focus on value for money

Whether you are trying to manage funding reductions, increased costs or challenges in achieving outcomes, you should be working with a proactive focus towards achieving value for money across all areas of the budget. 'Leading a School Budget Review' offers information on what schools can achieve from an in-depth review, and detailed advice on how to do it.

Broadly speaking, effective review of your school budget, at a high level to ensure financial sustainability and future viability, involves the following:

- Strategic leadership
- Understanding the context of your school
- Using financial data to inform change
- Leading teams
- Cultural change management
- Procedural and system change management
- Forecasting financial impact
- Monitoring and evaluating change

The process itself can be challenging, but is extremely important. Designating the most appropriate person to lead the review and allocating sufficient team capacity to support it are both critical to its success. You also need to allow for the time and effort it will take to make changes to systems, procedures and behaviours as a result of issues identified in the review.

There is a growing culture amongst schools, when faced with the challenge to 'do more with less', to think creatively and do things differently. The objective is, of course, to improve school performance continuously across many areas, which all ultimately impact on student outcomes. Financial constraints can have a negative impact, and often do when a 'salami slicing' approach is taken without an overarching focus on the vision. Schools that are able to rethink their strategy, coming up with creative solutions, can find the results they achieve to be even better than if they had maintained their original approach.

Key areas to consider reviewing to secure high savings are those which:

- represent a high proportion of overall budget spend, giving the potential for significant savings;
- involve third parties, such as contracts and services;
- are suspected or known areas of waste.

The following strategies are just examples of approaches that schools are taking to achieve savings. Please refer to our book 'Leading a School Budget

Review' for a more in-depth look at the full range of options.

Staff-related savings

Over time, discretionary expenditure has been cut as far as possible in many schools, leaving no option but to look at staffing, the biggest area. Many schools are now increasing class sizes and pupil:staff ratios, and reviewing how staff are deployed to maximise their contact time, making sure the rules are observed for planning, preparation and assessment (PPA) time.

Such a review might identify that some teachers are carrying out tasks which are not a good use of their time, and which could be done by support staff, freeing them up to focus on teaching and learning. At KS4 and 5, some subject options are being withdrawn as they are simply not viable.

It isn't unusual for the leadership team to be reviewed, and either re-sized or restructured, sometimes increasing contact time, and sharing responsibilities in a more cost-effective way. Teaching and Learning Responsibility (TLR) allowances can be reviewed across the school, although entitlements to protection mean that savings will only be fully achievable in the medium term.

Depending on local circumstances, you may be able to avoid compulsory redundancies by taking advantage of natural wastage, for example not replacing leavers and agreeing to requests from staff to move to part-time employment. This is not as easy as it sounds, particularly in secondary schools where subject coverage will be a concern, and where leavers are not always conveniently in the areas of curriculum surplus.

Across all types of staffing, think about changing working patterns to reflect when you need people around, especially if you are extending the school's activity at the beginning and end of the day or in holiday time, for example if the school is open for lettings and other use. You may need cover for reception and premises staff, for example.

In order to make sure new ways of working don't disrupt your school improvement journey, it is important to take a strategic view of staffing changes, re-imagining how you want to deliver the curriculum. Working with staff and unions will help restructuring if large-scale changes are needed.

The provider or commissioner debate

An area that is frequently debated is whether it is better to employ your own staff to deliver some services such as cleaning, caretaking, grounds maintenance and catering, or to go for contracted services with the local authority or a private provider. You can refer back to our section in chapter 11 on Supplies and Services for some of the issues with contracted services.

One way of exploring savings in existing contracts is to check that someone has been assigned responsibility for monitoring performance and triggering penalty charges if indicators are not achieved. Alternatively, you may decide to re-negotiate or re-tender a contract. If you do, make sure that you negotiate penalty clauses for under-performance to create a financial incentive for the supplier or provider to deliver quality goods or services.

You may decide to move from in-house services to contracted services. However, staff may have a legal right to transfer to the contractor - through the Transfer of Undertakings (Protection of Employment) Regulations, known as TUPE - and this can affect the cost of the contract.

If you are an academy, an honest conversation with suppliers about the pattern of payments can result in improvements to your cash flow, which is an important consideration for viability and can increase bank interest income. With so much competition for business, a company may be willing to show flexibility in order to keep your custom.

If you are unhappy with a contract, the idea of bringing the service in-house can be attractive, in the belief that you can recoup an LA's central overheads or a private company's profit margins. But depending on your local circumstances, you may have to observe different rules and conventions on staff pay, such as Single Status, a local Living Wage, and other terms and conditions of employment. You also need to consider the extra management responsibility, the provision and maintenance of specialist equipment (e.g. grass cutters and large-scale catering equipment) and running costs.

All these things can take up a surprising amount of time and incur a few headaches due to the peculiarities of some types of services. You will need supervisors who know all the legal requirements and there could be insurance implications. A contractor can cover fixed costs such as management and supervision across a number of contracts, but you will have to assess how much time to devote to these areas. On the other hand, you already have purchasing systems for equipment and consumables.

Having said all this, it may be possible to achieve savings by providing services in-house, compared to the contracts you are currently committed to. You will need to plan out a timescale for making this change as a self-contained project and take advice, particularly from people with legal and HR expertise, so you understand all the implications.

Income generation

Don't forget that savings are not only about reducing expenditure; they can also be achieved by increasing income. Refer back to our section in chapter 7 on ideas for income generation, but be careful not to be over-optimistic about how much extra income can be achieved, particularly in the early stages. It can take time to build up a customer base for commercial enterprises and the flow of income can be irregular.

Expanding the school

In an area of demographic growth, expansion could be an option for some schools. It all depends on whether you have physical space to accommodate extra pupils. A conversation with the LA Place Planning and/or School Organisation officer will be your first port of call, to establish whether there is a sustained demand in the local area or other plans such as a free school that will generate competition for the same pupils.

You can expect some resistance if you propose expansion where there isn't any growth in pupil numbers and where it may have a detrimental effect on nearby schools. This has the potential to cause tensions with your peers and create problems in collaborative working.

You will need to think through your expansion plans carefully. It is not as simple as increasing class sizes or creating new classrooms. There will be a knock-on effect in other respects. Can you continue to grow in terms of the overall school size, as more year groups have higher numbers? Can the extra management implications be absorbed within your current leadership structure? Will the extra pupils place more pressure on the school in terms of needs, such as SEND or additional needs related to deprivation, requiring more classroom support and not just an extra teacher?

Are the playing fields, assembly spaces, changing facilities, toilets, kitchen and dining hall facilities large enough to accommodate more pupils and get them all through the space in the required time, particularly for meals? Do you have enough car parking (the answer will invariably be no) for any extra staff that need to be recruited?

If none of these questions causes a problem, then it may be a viable way forward, creating a financial benefit if the extra funding exceeds the extra costs, for example by spreading your fixed costs over more pupils. But it needs to be a strategic decision, worked out in detail with senior staff, governors and the LA responsible for school place planning.

Overview - finding savings

Once budget areas are identified as having potential for savings, assigned teams can work on deep analysis of data and information to investigate and recommend actions. In our book, 'Leading a School Budget Review', we have provided bespoke templates with worked examples and checklists to support this work across pay and non-pay budgets.

Managed correctly, a review could lead to significant overall savings, either one-off or recurring. Depending on the fundamental objective of your budget review, these savings may support a deficit recovery plan, future financial sustainability or redirecting of resources to essential school improvement strategies. This will provide assurances to governors, trustees and external parties about the school's future viability and financial health.

Approval process

Once you achieve a budget you are satisfied with, you need to observe the approval processes. Only the full Governing Board can approve the budget of an LA maintained school. The Board of Trustees must approve a balanced budget for an academy. In both cases, the approval must be minuted.

In preparation for this, the Finance Committee should discuss the budget fully and explore all options before making a recommendation to the full Board. The School Business Leader and headteacher should provide supporting information for the most important areas, especially staffing.

What level of analysis is appropriate to present to the Board to enable them to ask the right questions before approving it? This is for the school to decide, bearing in mind that governors are not operational, but need sufficient detail to identify whether the proposed budget looks sensible.

LA schools generally use the Consistent Financial Reporting structure: https://www.gov.uk/guidance/consistent-financial-reporting-framework-cfr.

The DfE has published a chart of accounts for academies, as a standard for financial data. Adoption is voluntary, but enables automated data transfer from an academy trust's finance system to ESFA for financial returns. You can view it at https://www.gov.uk/government/publications/academies-chart of accounts.

Governors can request a more detailed breakdown of your budget if they want to explore particular areas of expenditure. What are the right questions that governors should ask to provide assurance that the budget is realistic and represents value for money?

As we mentioned in an earlier chapter, the DfE's 'Top Ten Planning Checks for Governors is excellent: https://www.gov.uk/guidance/school-resource-management-top-10-planning-checks-for-governors. It provides useful questions for governors to ask about staffing budgets, medium term projections, non-pay budgets, school improvement priorities and contracts.

We can't over-emphasise the importance of governor challenge in the budget setting process. It can feel like a daunting responsibility, but it is best for governors to follow their instincts when they think something doesn't sound right, and not worry too much about asking questions.

Challenge is an essential part of governance, and the headteacher and Chair of the Governing Board/Board of Trustees should consider how to encourage it. Using the local authority's governor clerking service can help, especially if training for governors is offered. Most services will place an emphasis on supporting governors to challenge appropriately. The Chair of Governors should also help other governors to undertake this role. Ofsted will look for evidence of challenge in all sorts of areas.

Watch out for future School Financial Success online training courses on finance for governors. All courses will be available through our website, at https://schoolfinancialsuccess.com/online-courses-2/.

Keeping the confidence of key stakeholders is important in preserving a positive profile for the school in the community, to help you retain a consistent level of admissions. While you will not want to divulge details of the school's finances beyond statutory requirements such as the statement on Pupil Premium, are there any high-level messages that you should give to parents to reassure them about the school's future financial stability?

Submitting your budget to funding bodies

Once the budget is finalised and approved by governors, you must submit it to your funding body by the relevant deadline.

The local Scheme for Financing Schools should outline the process for LA maintained schools to submit their budget, including timescales and the format. There may also be a local financial handbook. Academies should refer to guidance on submitting financial returns to ESFA at https://www.gov.uk/guidance/academies-financial-returns. This provides information on the deadlines for submission, including for new trusts.

Keeping the budget under review

The original budget is bound to change during the year. At one end of the scale, an Ofsted inspection could result in new priorities being identified, or your school might decide (or be forced) to convert to academy status. At the other, there may be opportunities to get a better deal on a contract, or you could be faced with staff turnover, sickness or maternity leave, requiring a different approach to the staff budget. You may have grouped together some expenditure on supplies and services under only a few headings, then decide to divide it up for a more detailed picture to help you monitor and control it.

To ensure an effective audit trail, you should always lock in an original budget version and record different versions as revised budgets in your budget software. You can then track the changes at a later date if required.

Recording the reasons for amending the budget will enable you to answer questions, prevent adjustments being done twice, and will be invaluable for new staff coming into post if you have turnover in key positions.

It is perfectly acceptable to move money between budget headings during the year. Local government has a technical term for this: virement (pronounced vy-er-ment). Indeed, it's essential if you need to cover an overspend in one area.

If you have identified a genuine need to increase a budget heading, you have two options:

- Take funding from the contingency, unless this would deplete it to a risky level. This can only be a one-off tactic, so if the overspend is likely to be repeated, you will need to identify a longer-term solution.
- Identify another cost centre where savings can be made, discuss it with the budget holder and transfer money from there to cover the overspend. If you don't do this, the budget holders who haven't spent all of their budget may think they can carry on spending it.

This needs a collegiate approach, so everyone understands it is not 'their' budget but the school's, and that the amount allocated may need to change over the course of the year in order to support the overall budget. We will cover this and more in the chapter on monitoring spending.

At all times, you need to regard your budget as dynamic, and keep an eye on the level of balances predicted at the year end. Prompt action on any areas of overspending will be essential, to avoid ending up in deficit.

13 MONITORING THE BUDGET

Principles of monitoring

Why do you need to monitor the budget? If you have taken every precaution to make it accurate, if it is in line with the school's activities, and with the majority of it being monthly salaries and contracts for goods and services, you'd think it would roll along quite nicely and need little attention.

Unfortunately, this is rarely the case. There will inevitably be changes to the best-laid plans, especially (but not exclusively) in a large school with a system of responsibility for budgets being devolved down to staff. You will probably have staffing changes such as leavers, maternity leave and sickness. You may have more pupils identified as having SEND, behavioural difficulties and other additional needs, who need different types of support.

You could experience turnover among budget holders, with new staff coming in who are not familiar with the assumptions underlying the budget. Even if they know the mechanics of managing a budget, without a knowledge of the culture of the school or the approach you have developed for this particular budget, it is possible that they may inadvertently waste resources.

When new senior staff are appointed, it is possible they may bring ideas which will help the school move more quickly towards meeting its priorities. Any related costs will need to be reviewed in line with resource capacity and any budget contingency.

You might have existing staff who have not had budget holding responsibilities before, and might make genuine mistakes, or overlook issues that affect their budget. It is important to provide training to new budget holders, tailored to their needs.

There might be obstacles that are not related to the behaviour of budget holders. Expenditure could be incorrectly coded through genuine mistakes by those placing orders on the system, or there could be unusual events that require additional spending such as problems with the building, and so on.

A budget is a strategic planning tool to ensure the school keeps its head above water financially and can achieve its aims. It is based on a set of intentions. However, it is the reality of your spending that will determine how much money you have (or don't have) at the end of the year. It is absolutely essential to keep on top of expenditure and income to make sure you are on track to achieve the planned level of balances at the end of the financial year.

If you are monitoring your expenditure and income regularly, you should pick up issues early enough to do something about them. If spending is allowed to run uncontrolled, it can derail the overall budget, causing problems for the whole school.

Perhaps the budget reflects plans for extra capacity in your staffing in a subject area that needs particular focus as part of a post-inspection action plan. In another area, you may need to bring in some expert support to address the under-performance of particular groups of pupils. Imagine some managers have sanctioned unexpected overtime claims for staff in a department, or a budget holder has ordered goods at a much higher specification or cost than is needed, not realising it will cause an overspend. A planned initiative might have to be cancelled if funding isn't available, due to other budget holders being unable to control their budgets. This could have a direct impact on those pupils' chances. It could also make an Ofsted grade's difference for the school.

School culture

The culture of the school is a major deciding factor in whether you keep to your budget or not. As we saw in the chapter on preparing the budget, staff engagement can make a real difference to your chances of achieving a balanced budget, but it can also help to make sure it stays that way throughout the year.

If it is a real team effort, with everyone pulling together to make sure financial controls are working effectively, school leaders and governors will feel supported and have greater confidence that any unexpected problems can be overcome. There will also be a greater sense of achievement across the school if your plans come to fruition, as everyone will feel they have played a part in the success.

Staff engagement will also encourage those with budget responsibilities to support each other. This has the benefit of reducing the demands on the School Business Leader, enabling them to focus on technical issues. We have already mentioned that proper training must be given to anyone taking on budget responsibilities for the first time, but refresher training should also be considered if some staff are struggling, or if there have been changes in areas such as the school's approach to managing the budget, a new financial system, academy conversion and so on. It's important to encourage colleagues to ask for support if they are having difficulties, and make them feel that their professional development is important. But make sure you prioritise your own development too!

In Chapter 9, we outlined the principles for creating the right culture for involving staff in preparing the budget. These principles also apply to budget monitoring, so please refer back to them. You simply need to find the approaches that are most effective in helping staff to realise when their decisions on spending might pose a risk to the budget.

Don't forget to celebrate achievements in keeping to the budget; this is not something to be taken for granted. It can often be difficult for budget holders to prioritise needs over 'wants'. The power of the shiny new thing can be very tempting! Try to take the same approach to recognising success in controlling budgets as you would to school improvement achievements; the impact on pupils of money being used wisely can be just as important. For that reason, it is equally important to tackle budget holders who persistently overspend. A quick check of year end results across the last three years should allow you to identify who they are.

One tactic to encourage prudent budget management is to introduce a managed underspend policy. This means that if a budget holder achieves a saving, they are allowed to carry it forward to the following year as an earmarked resource for their area. You would place a limit on this, e.g. 5% of the budget. What usually happens is that this provides an incentive to be cautious about spending, and budget holders can often save more than the upper limit for carrying forward. This can produce a win-win situation: your managers get an enhanced budget in the next year by carrying forward funds which you would have expected them to spend anyway, and you may get an unexpected extra saving in the budget overall, if they are ultra-cautious and over-achieve the carry-forward threshold.

Before going on to describe how to monitor your budget in detail, let's look at three different levels of monitoring - budget monitoring for governance purposes, internal high level review and budget holder detailed review. Each will be at a different frequency and for slightly different purposes, but all are important in order to achieve a robust approach to make the budget work as a whole.

Budget monitoring for governance purposes

Maintained schools must report budget monitoring information on a termly basis to governors through the lines of accountability set up within their organisation. This is likely to be to a Finance Committee which reports to the full governing body.

Academies must report budget monitoring information termly to local governing bodies but for MATs the process is much more stringent, with budget monitoring at whole trust level being reported to the Chair of the Trust Board twelve times per year and to all trustees six times per year. It is likely that this will be delegated to the Finance or Resources Committee.

The practice of termly budget monitoring should always include an outturn prediction, i.e. an estimate of the anticipated final position at the end of the financial year. Without this, there is no way for governors to interpret the current financial position in a meaningful sense. Telling governors how much of each budget is left at a particular point in the year can be misleading. It may appear that a substantial proportion of the budget is still available, and governors may assume it is heading towards an underspend, but won't be aware that some expenditure could be loaded towards the end of the year.

The bottom line of a predicted outturn report is a straightforward way to show governors whether the overall final school position is likely to be a surplus or a deficit. The penultimate column will draw attention to individual lines throughout the report that are not expected to be on target. There will be a mix of overspending and underspending, and it should be easy to identify the significant variations. The final column should provide an explanation of any significant variance which will help in responding to governor challenge when they ask why the variances have occurred.

We have made much of the need to link the school development plan with the budget, and this is also true in relation to monitoring performance against the budget. In discussing variations in expenditure and income, governors and leaders should make the link to any initiatives from the SDP that are included in the budget. They should be able to tell from the financial results how effective planned initiatives and actions have been, referring to any success criteria or performance indicators that have been set. Governors who are members of the Audit Committee should also be watchful of any recommendations from audit reports that impact on the budget.

As we've already seen, schools are not allowed to set planned deficit budgets without permission from their funding body, and it should be a priority to avoid going into deficit throughout the year. If an outturn prediction suggests this is a possibility, immediate changes must be made to the way the school is working and spending, to prevent it happening if at all possible. If regular budget monitoring for internal high-level review is being carried out effectively (as outlined below), there should not be any significant issues during the year that school leaders are not already aware of.

We've already mentioned that an 'Explanation of variance' column should be included in reports to governors. This is a text column explaining why a budget is over or under spent. It's a critical area for discussion. Significant over or under spends can suggest a lack of control, which should prompt governors to ask questions and challenge school leaders. In this way, the response to budget monitoring results is vital to achieving a value for money culture and high quality leadership and management of the budget.

We strongly advise schools to provide or buy in training to new governors and refresher training to the full Board periodically on the reading and interpretation of financial reports. This will save time in meetings and give governors more confidence in challenging the information. Governor challenge is a feature that Ofsted may look for in any desktop analysis either prior to or as part of inspection.

Budget monitoring for high level internal review

Budget monitoring at a whole school level is an essential tool for senior staff to reassure themselves that everything is running according to plan. The headteacher and senior finance staff should therefore undertake a regular internal review, ideally on a monthly basis.

This internal review will help to:

- avoid unnecessary overspending in specific budget areas
- inform ongoing school improvement planning
- manage unpredictable areas of the budget
- ensure input into the school finance system is accurate
- prepare for termly reports to governors, highlighting areas for discussion.

The essence of this type of monitoring is a high-level scanning of the main groupings of expenditure and income, to check that the overall budget is running reasonably well. It enables leaders to identify unexpected variances and drill down to find out the reasons for them. This will allow them to assess whether there is a risk of the overall budget being derailed.

It is important that this approach takes into account any known changes in the operation of the school, and tests out whether they are having an impact on the budget. For example, if there has been an Ofsted inspection, unforeseen staffing changes or an internal review of pupil performance, any agreed actions will need to be reflected in the budget, to make sure that resources are available for them. This might affect other areas of the budget, in which case decisions need to be taken on whether money has to be transferred from other cost centres that are underspending, or whether there are sufficient balances to accommodate the additional expenditure.

This process will feed into the termly reports to governors, enabling the headteacher and School Business Leader to decide which variances need to be drawn to the attention of governors.

Detailed monitoring for budget holders

As we have just seen, it is the responsibility of the headteacher and senior finance staff to monitor the overall budget for the school. But where responsibility for certain elements of the budget is devolved to budget holders, it is important that they undertake regular monitoring at a detailed level.

To monitor devolved budgets, accurate and timely information is essential. Budget holders need to be able to identify the total spending, including the value of orders placed, and check transactions have been recorded correctly. They will have many other responsibilities, so it needs to be as easy as possible for them to carry out their financial monitoring.

Finance staff should provide financial reports to budget holders on a monthly basis using the most up to date information from the finance system. Depending on your system capability and staff confidence, you could set up tailored reports on the system and train budget holders to run them whenever they wish, provided there is a reconciliation mechanism to check that everything has been included correctly from the most up to date records.

It is the responsibility of the budget holder to review their budget regularly, checking for accuracy in the expenditure and income that is recorded against their cost centre and comparing it with their own plans from the start of the year. Any budget holder should be able to predict whether their budget will be fully spent or not by the year end.

If there is a perceived risk of an overspend, finance staff should challenge this and encourage budget holders to review their spending and income, explain the reasons for the overspend and adjust their plans if necessary.

If an underspend is likely, budget holders should be encouraged to hold it in reserve to provide some flexibility in the budget as a whole, provided this will not cause problems in the planned delivery of activities or have a detrimental impact on achievement.

If there is an uncontrollable overspend in one part of the school's budget, it may be necessary to discuss with other budget holders ways of making savings in their devolved budgets, even if they have not caused the problem. If your culture is right, staff will not feel resentful about this; the money is not their personal fund but is something that has been entrusted to them.

The financial position of the whole school is everyone's responsibility. and ideally all staff will recognise that sometimes they need to give up some of their budgets for the greater good. They should have a reasonable expectation that if they run into genuine difficulties in the future that are outside of their control, they will benefit similarly from the collegiate approach. These discussions should take place with a shared awareness of the relative importance of priorities.

It is usually possible for finance systems to be set up in such a way that budgets cannot be overspent without high level authorisation from the School Business Leader or headteacher. This is not always the case; but whatever system you operate, it is the budget holder's responsibility to ensure their budget is not at risk of being overspent.

There should be continuous dialogue throughout the year between the finance team and budget holders, so that there are no surprises at the end of the financial year. Finance staff should be able to offer a more detailed analysis of spending and income at the budget holder's request, and should also be able to offer basic budget planning and monitoring training to budget holders where it is needed.

Budget holders are ultimately responsible for the budget they hold, so it is critical that monitoring is carried out regularly and that advice and guidance is sought from the finance team whenever needed.

14 INFORMATION FOR MONITORING

Information to support budget monitoring

It is essential that staff who are responsible for monitoring budgets understand the information that is provided to them. It is the basis on which conclusions will be drawn, so it must be timely, accurate, relevant and easy to follow. We have already discussed the format of the budget. Monitoring information should be presented using the same headings and it should be possible to drill down to lower levels of detail by requesting different reports from the school's financial system.

The first part of the process of budget monitoring at whole school level is comparing the actual expenditure and income plus known commitments against the latest version of the budget. This will help to identify any variance that is likely to occur at the year end.

In multi-academy trusts, the process and responsibility for monitoring budgets may vary. In some, the MAT will do most of the monitoring, and individual academies will only be required to provide information to identify reasons for variances compared to the budget. In others, there will be more delegated responsibility for monitoring at the individual academy level. It depends on the extent to which individual academies have responsibility for their own spending decisions; in many MATs, contracts for goods and services will be arranged centrally, for example. Some staff may work across the MAT and be funded from a central pot.

In all types of school, the biggest area to consider is staffing. Contractual information used to set the budget should have been accurate at that point, but there can be a range of changes during the year. The school will normally have a system that calculates the total expected cost (including on-costs for NI and pension contributions) from individual staff contracts. It will reconcile charges from the payroll system, so you can verify what is charged to your budget by your payroll provider. It is essential that this is kept under close scrutiny and that adjustments are made to the budget for any changes that affect pay expenditure, such as pay awards, starters, leavers, pay progression, allowances or staff opting out of the pension scheme.

At all times, you should be aware of the impact of staffing changes on your budget, and if necessary take action to reduce other expenditure to balance the overall budget.

A more detailed approach is needed at an individual budget holder level, since it forms the foundation of budgetary control. As with any process that builds on low-level checking, if this aspect isn't right, the overall achievement of your goals could be put at risk. The next sections therefore cover the basics of how processing of expenditure works, so that those who might not be familiar with the details do not make inaccurate assumptions about how costs are charged to budget headings. If you are not involved at this level, feel free to skip this section, or skim it to get a basic understanding.

Processing of expenditure

The process of recording expenditure in the accounts has several steps:

- When an order is placed on the financial system, it is recorded in the system as a commitment. This can be a known value (preferably) or can be estimated.
- When the invoice is received and logged on the system, it cancels out the commitment (order value) and the actual amount is recorded as expenditure.
- When the invoice is paid from the school's bank account, this doesn't affect the monitoring reports, as it goes on behind the scenes. Only the finance staff need to look at this. Cash flow, in other words the net effect of funding coming in and payments going out in a particular period (usually monthly) is a particularly important issue for academy finance staff.

You can see the importance of trying to include reasonably accurate costs on an order, given that they will be built into budget monitoring reports until payment is made. Budget holders should normally be expected to find out the actual cost before placing an order, but there may be some legitimate reasons why this is not possible. If this is the case, in most financial systems there will usually be an option to hide the price on the version that goes to the supplier, if you don't want them to see your estimated price.

Now you understand the basics of how expenditure hits the accounts, let's look in a little more detail at the importance of commitments on the system.

Financial commitments

Generally, your budget monitoring reports will show expenditure to date plus known commitments that should turn into expenditure by the year end.

If you have a dynamic management information system with linked HR and Finance modules, the pay lines on your budget monitoring report can include salary commitments. These represent the expected salary costs for the remainder of the year. These are only reliable if staff contracts are kept up to date in the HR module. If you don't have an integrated system, you will need to input information as part of month end work and monitor salary commitments manually.

In non-pay lines on the report, commitments will show up where goods and services have been ordered but invoices haven't yet been received from the supplier. Commitments are derived from the amount recorded on orders that have been placed. It is therefore important to make sure that they are completely cancelled out when invoices are received, otherwise they will remain part of your total expenditure, overstating it. This is undesirable because you might erroneously assume you have an overspend and may hold back on a project that would have been beneficial to pupil outcomes.

There are several reasons why a commitment might stay on the system longer than expected:

- the goods or services haven't been delivered yet, so payment isn't due;
- the goods or services have been delivered, but the invoices haven't yet been received and/or paid;
- the goods and services were delivered, but were not what was ordered or not up to standard and have been returned. There will be no invoice and the order needs to be cancelled. Sometimes an order might be partly fulfilled, with some items missing or returned. In both cases, the remaining commitments will need to be removed manually if you are not going to receive or keep the goods.
- the goods and services have been delivered and an invoice has been received and entered on the system, but the amount was lower than the price recorded on the order. This residual amount may just sit there unless it is cancelled.

Budget holders should be strongly advised not to place orders by telephone or online unless they have authorisation and an audit trail such as an email receipt, which can be passed to the finance team for entry on the system.

Orders that haven't yet been replaced by invoices will be recorded in the commitments column within budget monitoring reports, and added to the actuals column to produce a total expenditure figure. The inclusion of the commitment in these reports underlines the importance of accurately estimating the cost of an order. Budget holders should let finance staff know if the order isn't going to be fulfilled, or if the initial value isn't accurate, so that they can cancel the unwanted commitment.

There may also be regular payments (sometimes called periodic payments) such as subscriptions to services, software, publications and so on. These can occur monthly, quarterly, termly, six-monthly or annually at different times of the year. The larger periodic payment items like energy bills and ICT software licences will probably be managed centrally by the finance team.

It is good practice for finance staff to run a monthly housekeeping exercise for committed expenditure on the finance system to ensure anything that shouldn't be there is cancelled, and check that there are commitments for all known orders. This will involve liaison with budget holders to ensure the correct decision is made with regard to the commitment.

While it is important for budget holders to notify finance staff of orders that won't result in an invoiced payment, if this doesn't happen it should be picked up at the year end. As part of the closure of accounts process, there should be an exercise to cancel off old orders that are still on the system, so they don't continue to show up as a commitment against the budget.

We will now look at the importance of tidying up systems at the year end.

Expenditure that crosses financial years

Towards the year end, finance staff will keep a careful eye on any significant expenditure where goods and services have been received but where invoices have not yet arrived. They will need to make sure the expenditure is charged to the correct financial year, via a system called accruals. If you are a budget holder, you don't need to worry about this as the finance team will handle it, but you should ensure there are good lines of communication between you to reduce the potential for anything to be missed. To enable you to do this, we offer an explanation of the process.

For expenditure to count against the financial year, goods and services must have been received by the end of it. This can affect the performance against budget if purchases cross over the end of the financial year and end up being charged to the new year instead of the old year.

Let's use two examples for a local authority school whose financial year ends at the end of March.

- **Scenario 1**: an order is placed in February but the goods or services aren't delivered until April, and the invoice is received after that. The expenditure will be charged to the new year and no adjustment is necessary, since payment is in the same year the items were received.
- **Scenario 2**: an order is placed in February and the goods or services are delivered in March, but the invoice doesn't arrive until April. When the invoice is paid, it will be charged to the new year, but the school can arrange for it to be moved back to the old year (subject to the note below on materiality) because that was when the goods or services were received.

As long as the goods are in school or the service has been delivered before the year end, the cost can be charged back to the old year, regardless of when payment is made. This charge is called an 'accrual'. For those with a finance background, it places a debit in the old year to record the expenditure, and a credit in the new year to cancel out the subsequent payment of the invoice.

If these adjustments aren't made, the accounts will show an underspend in the old year but an unexpected overspend in the new year. The ability to carry balances forward means this isn't normally a problem, but in another sense, it can lead to erroneous assumptions, for example if you are trying to look at trends in expenditure and don't realise that something is being charged to a different year.

It's worth bearing in mind that auditors will look at materiality (the significance of the values involved), recommending that adjustments between years are only done for higher value items to avoid causing a lot of work. For smaller items, it's hardly worth the effort to do transfers between years, because balances will be slightly higher as a result of the mismatch and this will fund the expenditure in the new year.

Usually this only applies to a relatively small proportion of expenditure, so it won't cause much disruption to the year end result. But it's worth being aware of it and checking the practice with finance staff. If you have a significant purchase that falls into Scenario 2, you will want to make sure this is transferred back to the old year, because it could make a hole in your budget allocation for the new year.

Processing of income

Income is recorded either when the school issues a debtor's invoice to the person that has received goods or a service from you, or when a customer makes a cash payment that you haven't sent an invoice for. There will be a difference in timing of the money hitting your account: as soon as you produce the debtor's invoice on the system, it will generate an income record, even though the customer hasn't paid you yet. But non-invoiced cash payments will only be credited to your account when you bank the money.

Many schools use cashless online systems or cards to collect payments for meals and school trips, in which case the money will be transferred into your bank account electronically. A member of the finance team will usually be responsible for checking this and matching up all the income against what is expected, making sure it is allocated to the correct code. Budget holders who generate income are advised to check that it shows up against their budget, in case it has gone to someone else's!

Wherever possible, you should collect payments up front before delivering the service, to minimise the risk of non-payment and extra work in chasing debts. If you send someone a debtor's invoice but they do not pay it and all attempts to recover the money fail, at some point you will need to write it off. This means the income will have to be removed from your income heading. If you have budgeted for it, a debt you haven't recovered produces the same effect as an overspend.

One of the areas you may decide to improve in order to address a budget shortfall could be to sharpen up financial procedures. Particular areas to consider may include reconciling income to make sure everything that is collected ends up in the right place, and ensuring that you have all the relevant customer details when sending out invoices, making it easier to chase up those who don't pay what they owe.

Analysis and interpretation

Where spending in a specific area of the non-pay budget is approaching the total budget more quickly than you expected, you need to question why.

The first consideration is whether items are being miscoded. The information may not be accurate, and you could be being charged for someone else's purchases. A simple exercise will sort this out and put it back on track. It is always easier to arrange clear communications between finance staff and budget holders in the first place, so that the correct codes are used from the start of the financial year, rather than have to pick up errors and put them right at various points during the year. Don't waste scarce resources by allowing careless mistakes to take up precious staff time; it's easy enough to prepare a list of cost centres with examples of the sort of expenditure that should go under each, and encourage budget holders and those processing orders to ask if they're not sure.

If you are confident the items charged to each heading are accurate, another layer of questions come into play:

- Was the original budget an accurate prediction?
- Have prices increased beyond what was originally anticipated?
- Are more goods being purchased, or more of the service being used, than originally intended?
- What is the impact on outcomes? Is the overspend justified or deliberate?
- Do you want this area of spending to continue at this rate and if so, will other areas of the budget need to be adjusted?
- If you don't want the spend to continue at this rate, what needs to be done about it?

The last question opens up a range of options. Some will be one-off in nature ('quick-fix'), but others will prompt action to achieve longer-term changes ('stay-fix'). If you find a lot of time is being spent addressing the same problems, it's an indication that you need to be more proactive in getting to the root of the issue and making pre-emptive changes.

An example of stay-fix thinking is asking whether the school policy needs to be reviewed in order to trigger the change needed. For example, your school policy may allow school trips to run in school time, but the supply budget may be using up too much of the original budget and a significant overspend looks likely. Should the school policy be changed? You could decide that trips should either run outside normal hours or in holiday time when no supply is needed, or be led by support staff to reduce supply costs.

If the spend in a specific budget area is not progressing towards the total budget set as quickly as you expected it to, you still need to question why. Are these goods or services no longer needed? If so, you would expect a genuine underspend at the year end. Will the spend occur later in the year? That is more likely to be a matter of different timing of expenditure and the budget will be fully used up by the year end. The answers to these questions will help you to decide if this area of the budget can be used to offset another where an overspend is likely.

Not all expenditure is in regular monthly or even termly amounts. Watch out for areas with irregular spending. You may need to pay a lump sum at a particular point in the year, for items such as subscriptions and exam fees. Understanding cost patterns (also known as the expenditure profile) will help in assessing whether the monitoring information gives cause for concern.

Informing school improvement planning

It is essential to produce year end projections as part of regular budget monitoring. This makes you focus on areas where changes could pose a risk, identifying problems at an early stage and enabling prompt action to be taken to resolve them. Understanding why costs vary and seeing areas of weakness in financial control will enable you to tighten up procedures and tackle staff behaviour where financial responsibilities aren't being discharged effectively.

The year-end projections will inform decisions on spending and school improvement planning for the remainder of the year. You may need to adjust some expenditure plans to cover unexpected overspending in other areas. Knowledge of problems in the current year will raise awareness of areas of risk when preparing the following year's budget.

Some specific issues may arise in relation to school improvement strategies and performance outcomes. You may need to respond to unexpected exam results, adjusting priority areas to tackle under-performance in certain areas. Proactive assessment will identify groups of children who are not progressing as they should, and you need to know whether there are any spare pots of money which can be used to provide intensive tuition in the relevant subject areas to help them catch up.

As a result of regular budget monitoring and financial predictions, school leaders may need to move money from one budget area to another, or even review school policy. Budget monitoring should work in conjunction with the regular review of the SDP as part of the school improvement planning cycle. This will involve school leaders rigorously questioning and challenging themselves to ensure that resources continue to be available and are targeted in a way that meets the school's improvement priorities. Where this is not the case, changes to the SDP may be necessary, in an attempt to cause as little detrimental effect to pupil outcomes as possible.

15 CHALLENGES IN BUDGET MONITORING

Managing unpredictable areas of the budget

How do you manage budgets effectively, when the nature of the expenditure means you have no idea what is coming from one day to the next?

Premises costs

In our chapter on budget preparation, we looked at the challenges of setting premises budgets. You will have made your best estimate at the start of the year about how much to set aside based on certain assumptions, but this area often presents a heightened risk of veering away from your plans.

Repairs and maintenance is one of the more unpredictable areas of expenditure within a school budget. There is no getting away from the fact that an unexpected fault with plant, machinery, or building systems can happen at any time and sometimes at great expense.

It is unlikely that you will have been able to predict these sorts of incidents; moreover, if you have financial difficulties, it is unwise to hold resources in specific budget lines for events that might not happen. It is better to aim for an overall level of contingency within the budget that can be applied to cover any unexpected and unavoidable spending as it occurs.

Measures can be taken to reduce the risk of unpredictability in premises expenditure, although they will not mitigate against it completely. Some of the more common budget management tactics are detailed below:

a. **Insurance**

- If you have any damage or theft, check your policies carefully to ensure you make a claim when it is appropriate to do so, to avoid an unnecessary charge against your budget.
- Be aware of any policy excess which might make it less economic to make a claim, especially if it will affect future premiums.
- All schools have the opportunity to be part of the DfE's Risk

Protection Arrangement (RPA) insurance scheme.

b. Maintenance schedule

- Ensure all plant, equipment and machinery in school is regularly maintained and tested. This is essential for health and safety but also wise to ensure optimum performance and reduce the risk of fault through lack of service or irregular maintenance checks. These tests may highlight unexpected work that is needed.
- Follow advice from the experts you employ to carry out the maintenance, and if you are not sure about remedial action and need a second opinion, seek advice from specialists within your LA/MAT team or from other schools who may have experienced similar issues.

c. Monitoring

- The Repairs and Maintenance budget should be monitored in detail, on at least a monthly basis. Detailed analysis and consideration of issues regularly throughout the year will help you to make critical decisions regarding the running of the school to ensure a high-quality learning environment.

If your school has had a Private Finance Initiative (PFI) build or a Building Schools for the Future (BSF) contract, you may have a Sinking Fund held by the local authority which is designed to cover future repairs and refurbishments. The school will make annual contributions to the Sinking Fund; these won't necessarily be at a consistent level throughout the length of the contract. Any repairs which meet pre-agreed criteria, such as 'end of life', are paid for by withdrawing money from the fund. Although there are disadvantages to PFI contracts, particularly their inflexibility and an inability to make savings from them, one benefit is that you can avoid sudden significant expense when repairs or refurbishment is needed in a single year, because it is covered by the fund that you have paid into.

Energy budgets can also be unpredictable. It is particularly important to monitor usage, charges and the timing of bills. If the local authority manages a bulk contract for energy, watch out for adjustments which can sometimes take an inordinate amount of time to process. If you are lucky, this could result in a refund for several years of over-payments, but the alternative is more unpalatable: a significant one-off charge to your budget that causes an unexpected overspend.

Anything unexpected like this is highly undesirable from a planning point of view. It is always worth getting in touch with the Energy Management team at the local authority to verify the timings of payments and check whether bills are being paid on estimates or meter readings. Having a contingency to cover issues such as this is very important.

You may be sharing part of your building with other organisations and the arrangements for cost sharing might include estimated usage of energy. Think about whether there is a fair split, or whether the organisation uses more or less energy than the school, in which case the agreement should reflect this.

Supply cover

You might be able to plan ahead for absences such as maternity leave, but you may see a mixture of other short, medium and longer term absences that you couldn't possibly have predicted when setting the budget. A provision for supply cover based on previous years' estimates is a good starting point.

You can find the DfE's deal for an approved list of supply agencies at https://www.gov.uk/guidance/deal-for-schools-hiring-supply-teachers-and-agency-workers.

It may be tempting to build in a contingency, particularly if this is an area of your budget which has suffered an overspend in the past. But as with repairs and maintenance, if you have financial difficulties, it is unwise to hold resources in specific budget lines for events that might not happen.

Common tactics to reduce the risk of unpredictability for supply cover costs include:

a. Cover Supervisors

The direct employment of cover supervisors, who are available to cover lessons when required and work flexibly across other areas of need during quieter times, is becoming more commonplace. Since these staff understand how the school works and are known to the pupils, they may offer high quality support and a more consistent approach than a series of agency staff who are unknown to the school. Alternatively, some agencies now offer cover supervisors, as well as qualified teachers. They are charged at a lower daily rate and are an ideal solution for covering short term absence.

b. Staff Absence Insurance

This can be very useful for schools with a high level of absence. Make sure you understand the criteria for claims and terms and conditions of the policy before committing to any agreements. It is important to understand how your level of claims will affect premiums in future years and regularly monitor whether the arrangement is providing value for money. If the premium costs more than the value of claims made each year, you may decide against insurance. However, it is important to be aware of the risks of doing this, if you subsequently change your mind. When an insurer first accepts your business, they will exclude staff with pre-existing conditions/illnesses and may build in higher costs because you represent an unknown risk, even though you will be asked to provide a history of absences.

c. Staff Well-being

Not all absences are due to illness, but using the data and information available to you from your management information system will help you to identify if this is a cause for concern for your school. Staff wellbeing programmes offer a positive and proactive solution to support staff health and well-being. This can improve staff performance and ultimately reduce absence levels. Not only is this good financial sense in terms of avoiding high supply cover costs, it also represents very good value for money, as the impact on the students of happy, motivated and highly performing teachers is measurable.

Staff recruitment

Staff advertising to support recruitment can also be an unpredictable area to manage. You may think you have a stable staffing structure one year, but you might then experience a higher than normal turnover of staff the following year. Schools with pupil performance challenges may be expecting to spend more in this area in order to attract and recruit talented staff to support their drive for improvement.

Schools with an older staff age profile might be able to plan ahead to some extent, but retirement age is now so variable that this is still a difficult task. Even schools that consider themselves to have a solid staffing complement and believe that they offer a desirable place to work may experience staff movement outside of their control, for instance if staff members decide to relocate due to family circumstances.

There are now lots of free resources that can be used to market your staff vacancies. Your existing school website is the perfect starting point. Make sure it is attractive and eye-catching as well as informative and compliant. Consider developing an area of your website solely for recruitment purposes, accessible from the homepage. This allows you to sell your school to future employees, detailing why your area is an attractive place to live and work as well as your school's unique selling point. You are presenting a different angle to that used for your two main website audiences, parents and pupils.

Other free resources can be found in your local area with a little bit of research. Often online services for advertising can be completely free of charge or carry a small annual charge which covers unlimited use.

For more expensive advertising packages, such as in well-known educational publications, consider a recruitment package deal. There are different options to suit the needs of different schools. Often paying for a package in advance will bring significant savings compared to paying for successive single advertisements. The best package deals offer a rolling set-up, so that if you don't use your pre-paid adverts in one year, they are automatically rolled over to the next.

Accurate input into finance system

A school's financial procedures should include instructions and guidance on the use of finance systems and accurate coding lists (the chart of accounts). These are designed to ensure that school finance staff input codes correctly when carrying out financial transactions on the system. Even with highly competent and well trained staff and detailed and accurate procedures in place, mistakes can be made that can result in postings to incorrect codes.

Miscodings can frustrate your attempts to control the budget. They create a false impression of how well you are achieving the targets you've set for spending and income. If you rely on the figures presented without checking for errors, you might draw invalid conclusions, and set an inaccurate budget for the following year which could cause problems.

The monthly exercise of budget monitoring allows for a detailed review of the budget at whole school level, which can often highlight any incorrect postings in the previous month. Journals can then be processed to correct any mistakes and action can be taken to ensure that future reports are accurate and meaningful.

Ideally the senior member of the finance team undertaking the monthly budget monitoring exercise will not be involved in daily transaction processing. This allows for a segregation of duties and quality assurance of the finance processes carried out.

16 FINANCIAL TARGETS IN APPRAISAL

Staff accountability

You may have spotted a theme in this book, which is the importance of shared financial responsibility as a pre-requisite for effective financial leadership in successful schools. When you consider the current prospects for school budgets, creative thinking could make the difference between just surviving and thriving.

Whilst the Senior Leadership Team should lead the way, there are huge benefits in a shared responsibility filtering down to all staff, to embed a strong culture of value for money with everyone travelling in the same direction.

Encouraging a value for money culture

Formal external accountability for financial leadership in schools usually sits with the Headteacher and School Business Leader (SBL), with involvement of all leaders being essential for success. Internal accountability of the wider staff for their role, contribution and shared responsibility for financial leadership can be more variable, with some schools demonstrating this better than others and some staff responding to the challenges with more enthusiasm than others.

We recognise the challenges in building a school culture where every member of the school community is mindful of avoiding waste and making the most of the resources available to support quality education. Even if a message is repeated regularly, you cannot guarantee everyone will hear and understand it, particularly in large organisations where the message can be diluted the further down the line from the headteacher it goes.

In this chapter, we would like to offer a practical solution to kick-start that journey, through the strategic use of performance objectives to develop a culture of respect for each other, the environment we learn in and the resources we use. Our advice is suitable for any school regardless of size, status, phase or specialism and is a foundation for you to adapt and build on to make it work for you in the context of your school.

Our concept is to interweave a strong message for shared financial leadership through performance objectives for teaching and support staff at any level. This doesn't mean compromising on objectives relating to student outcomes for teachers, and it doesn't mean applying generic objectives that are meaningless to some support staff due to the many variations of roles in a school. This is an idea that can work for everyone, at every level and pay your school back in abundance if you get it right.

Financial targets for teacher appraisal

Let's start by considering teaching staff appraisal. Once referred to as 'performance management' but now termed 'appraisal', this is the recurring annual process of holding teaching staff to account for their performance.

Appraisal objectives are set at the beginning of the academic year at a meeting between the appraiser and appraisee. Progress towards the objectives is measured at an interim meeting part way through the year. A final meeting towards the end of the academic year finalises evidence and leads the appraiser to make a recommendation to the Headteacher in relation to the appraisee's potential for movement up the pay range.

The Headteacher reviews all evidence, takes the appraiser's recommendation into account and makes their own recommendation to governors regarding pay levels for every teacher, through the annual Pay Review process. The now more stringent policy of performance related pay adds greater importance to this process. Every teacher must evidence their improved performance through this process to secure any movement through the pay range, not just at the threshold level, as was the case before the introduction of performance related pay in 2014.

A lot is riding on this process for the individual and for the school. If the process isn't right, teachers could be underpaid or overpaid and disagreements over decisions could lead to appeals, hearings and a negative impact on staff morale as well as a demand on leadership time. Support, training and advice should be in place for all staff and particularly directed to those who are not successful in meeting their objectives. It is also clear that objectives must link to learners' learning and progress, as this is the main measure of a school's success.

But a school's results are only sustainable if the school is financially viable in the future. High standards in a school with a serious deficit are built on shifting sands and may not be maintained if significant cuts have to be made.

Financial health and sustainability aims are thus just as important as educational objectives and are growing in profile under the current pressures.

It therefore seems appropriate to reflect the importance of financial sustainability in setting objectives for appraisal where staff have a responsibility for an aspect of the school's financial performance.

Unions suggest a maximum of three annual appraisal objectives for teaching staff. Most schools apply this concept and whilst there may be some variation, two or three objectives are common. As more than one objective is set for each teacher, it seems logical that one or two objectives could be focused on learner outcomes and one focused on shared financial leadership.

This still allows scope for learner outcome-related objectives spanning more than one area, e.g. a KS4 and KS3 objective for secondary teachers, or objectives related to the progress and attainment of different student cohorts, e.g. boys, pupils eligible for Pupil Premium, SEND pupils, or more able and talented. The balance between objectives can be tailored depending on whole school priorities and team priorities of individual teachers.

Securing one objective for financial leadership raises the profile of this important agenda in your school with very little effort. You must make sure you get the wording right and that the objective works for the person's level of responsibility, but beyond that the hard work is already done for you. The teacher will realise the level of importance you are placing on this because the evidence of their contribution to this priority will link to their potential for pay progression. The process for holding to account, providing and recording evidence is already in place through your appraisal set-up.

Financial leadership objectives

So, what might a teacher's 'financial leadership' appraisal objective look like? We already know objectives need to be SMART (Specific, Measurable, Achievable, Realistic, and Timely). We are now open to the concept that at least one objective could relate to financial leadership and we also understand the importance of the objective wording being relevant to the teacher's level of responsibility.

Use the table on the next page for some ideas which could be offered during the appraisal process to link financial leadership objectives to teacher level.

Senior leaders	Teach the concept of value for money (VfM) to others in your application of it by role modelling behaviour, explaining the reasons for financial decisions and challenging others to make decisions on the same basis. How can you evidence the financial impact of decisions you have taken or contributed to? How can you evidence opportunities taken to be a role model for appropriate financial behaviour?
Middle leaders/TLR budget holders	Consider how efficiently members of your team use their time and resources to support the priorities of your faculty/area. Does spending relate back to your faculty development plan? Are team members using their time wisely to focus on team priorities? How can you evidence value for money as the basis of the financial decisions you make?
Budget holders	Prepare an achievable and realistic spending plan for your budget area which is clearly linked to your development plan, enabling the priorities that have been set to be achieved within the budget limit you have been allocated. How will you monitor progress against the plan throughout the year? How can you evidence value for money as the basis of the financial decisions you make?
All teachers	Consider how efficiently you use resources to support your teaching and learning strategies. How can you improve your approach to reduce waste, potentially save money and most importantly not compromise on impact?

Financial targets for support staff

It is good practice to have an equivalent process for support staff in schools, but this is not statutory because appraisal for these staff is not linked to pay. The pay structures for support staff are completely different from those for teaching staff.

Teaching is a profession where individuals can build on their fundamental teaching experience and expertise over time and increase their level of leadership responsibility, contributing to potential movement through the pay range and potential additional payments. However, it is fundamentally one profession with teaching and learning at the core. If you take any additional responsibilities out of the picture, performance of this core and shared function can be measured, creating a fair system of salary movement to reflect performance over time.

Support staff roles in schools are many and extremely varied. This one label of 'support staff' encompasses a plethora of roles which can be manual, administrative or directly related to teaching and learning support, with many more variations in between. It is a complex set-up which is essential for school success, with support staff being ever more valued and relied upon for their critical contributions.

Pay for support staff roles can, in theory, be compared to equivalent roles outside of education. The NJC pay scales provide ranges of points in a grading structure, allowing for automatic movement up the pay scale over time, within the grade set for a role. The range of the grade is often limited to three incremental points, particularly at the lower end of the pay scale.

When the top of a grade is reached, that member of staff will stay at the same point, unless their role changes or additional responsibility is given, sufficient to warrant a grade promotion. This is very different to the set-up for teachers.

Whilst we may understand why a support staff appraisal process is not linked to pay, it does make it more difficult for school leaders to motivate these staff to buy into any equivalent process. Recognising and celebrating success is a motivator which helps to get that buy-in. A letter from the Headteacher at the end of the appraisal process, congratulating individual staff on what they have achieved, can have a positive impact on morale. It is good for school culture if strategies such as these are adopted for all staff. For teachers, a paragraph could be incorporated into the more formal letters which accompany the teacher appraisal process.

Many schools have a process in place for support staff that is equivalent to appraisal, which may be referred to using varying terminology. For our purposes, let's call it a 'development review'.

The purpose of a development review for support staff is to encourage improved and sustained high performance and maintain a focus on continuous learning, development and training. It can support those who may be looking to further their role in the future and it can support those who want to get better in, or continue to do well in, their current role.

The objectives set are critical to the success of any development review.

Some level of ownership from the individual is important, but there is also an opportunity for school leaders to guide the development of the support staff body.

Objectives should be:

- Focused
- linked to whole school priorities and team priorities
- relevant to the role
- relevant to the responsibility level
- SMART (Specific, Measurable, Achievable, Realistic, Timely)

As with teaching staff, an appraiser should be appointed to every individual member of support staff and the process should mirror the arrangements for teaching staff in terms of frequency and focus of meetings throughout the year. The appraiser would report the outcomes of the meetings to a central point, possibly the SBL or HR manager whose responsibility it is to ensure that sufficient support is being offered to enable all support staff to meet their objectives, including meeting any training needs.

The complexity in relation to support staff is caused by the many different types of role which make up the support staff team. If you are looking to offer a series of objectives for support staff to use, you would in theory need many permutations to suit everyone. You also need to think about the level staff are working at, to ensure objectives are suitably challenging. This is where we think we can help, with a baseline idea which you can adapt to suit your own circumstances.

Consider drawing an imaginary line at a point on the support staff pay scale you use, that separates those staff you consider to be at a manager or leader level. You won't necessarily end up with an even split on either side of the line but you should be comfortable that those at the higher end, above your line, are roles that you would expect to have more challenging development objectives.

All staff should agree either two or three objectives with their appraiser at their first development review meeting. Staff on the lower grades you have identified should agree a minimum of two objectives, with an optional third objective. Staff on the higher grades, above the line, should agree three objectives. The following table provides a suggested grouping of objectives.

Ref	Objective	Relevant to
1	A personal professional development objective to be agreed by appraiser and appraisee	All staff on scheme
2	To be selected from operational section	All staff on scheme
3	To be selected from leadership section	e.g. Grades C-F (optional) e.g. Grades G and above (compulsory)

This sort of structure is just an example and needs to be applied to your own pay scale.

You now need to develop a series of objectives which fit into two sections. The operational section will be at a level you feel is challenging enough for lower grades and the leadership section will reflect the responsibilities of staff on higher grades.

In reality, not all of the objectives you set will be directly related to financial management, but you can focus some in this area to raise the profile of shared financial leadership. Depending on the circumstances of your school, you may want to make it compulsory for staff to select at least one objective which has a financial focus. Remember also that saving staff time, improving staff productivity and working more efficiently are all aspects of a value for money culture that can be developed.

Examples of objectives in the operational section are outlined below:

Use of resources:

Identify the potential for efficiency savings and/or waste reduction in your area of work and suggest strategies to realise these, working with your line manager to support implementation where appropriate.

Discuss the importance of value for money with your appraiser and/or line manager.

How will you evidence your impact?

Communication and shared working:

Identify ways to improve communication in your team to ensure efficient working practices, maximise productivity and reduce waste.

For example, this could involve:

- considering how well your area of the network is used to share information and resources
- reducing team printing and photocopying and finding alternative solutions to share information amongst stakeholders

Examples of objectives in the leadership section are shown below.

Change management:

Improve systems and/or working practices, within your area of work, to ensure staff efficiency and/or secure financial savings.

Any proposed change must be discussed and agreed with your appraiser and your line manager in advance.

Will the change impact on school culture? How will you manage this?

Have you thought about appropriate training and support for colleagues?

Are there resource implications to consider? (If so, ensure budget holder approval is sought in advance)

How will you measure and evidence the impact of the change?

Leadership:

Support a team member or whole team to develop their financial leadership skills.

Identify a potential development/improvement within your area of work which supports the school's financial leadership and value for money culture. Lead a team member or whole team to make improvements to working practices. Think about:

- Support
- Motivation
- Coaching

How will you measure and evidence your impact?

Can you get feedback from your colleagues to enhance your evidence, e.g. using 'What Went Well' (WWW) and 'Even Better If' (EBI) technique.

The key to success is to make use of our suggestions within the context of your own school. You may be able to lift some of our examples and use them directly. Others may not fit in the context of your priorities or school set-up, but hopefully they will give you an idea of the thought process, so that you can develop your own objectives that would suit your staff in your own school's context.

17 STRATEGIC FINANCIAL PLANNING

Key elements of strategic financial planning

Your most immediate concerns about your school's finances are likely to be the current year's performance against budget, which will determine how much money you will have left at the end of the year, and your ability to balance next year's budget. But it is equally as important to undertake strategic financial planning, so that you have a blueprint to follow for the years after that.

What does strategic financial planning mean?

In Chapter 2, we talked about strategic financial leadership, defining it as creating a vision for how the available resources will be used to achieve your school's aims in the longer term, and implementing that vision in a way that creates the conditions for sustainable improvement.

Strategic financial planning is a sub-set of this, looking at organising the use of your resources at a high level across a multi-year period, always making sure you have enough money, and that you spend it well.

What does spending it well mean? Essentially, it means that you are targeting the resources you have to the school's priorities, i.e. the things that are important to you, your staff and above all your pupils. What is important should always be the things that work best to achieve your aims. Financial decisions need to be rooted in evidence as to which strategies have the biggest impact on outcomes.

This doesn't mean planning a precise budget for a five-year period. The best you could say is that any attempt to do this will be wrong. But you should have a sense of the overall shape of what resources might be available, and how they will be spent. After all, your high-level strategic priorities are unlikely to change fundamentally; it's only the detail that might change, for example in response to national decisions on performance measures or local circumstances.

In our view, the key elements of strategic financial planning are:

a) Linking the budget to the School Development Plan and school improvement planning cycle
b) Multi-year budget planning
c) Projecting future rolls
d) Undertaking a budget review if faced with financial challenges
e) Planning ahead for potential staffing reductions
f) Always keeping in mind the potential for income generation to maximise the resources available

We have already covered items d) and e) from the above list in Chapter 12 (Finalising the budget) and item f) in Chapter 7 (Finding sources of income), so our focus in the rest of this chapter will be on the first three. This will give you a firm strategic foundation so you can avoid the need for a major budget review, which might require reductions in staffing.

The benefits of strategic financial planning

So far, we've shown you the process for setting and monitoring the annual budget. This is the foundation for making the best use of resources. But taking one year at a time will only get you so far. A vision isn't just for one year; it's a long-term position, a strategic intention that will be pursued for some years to come.

Strategic financial planning is another vital part of your toolkit for making the best use of your funding to maximise outcomes for pupils. It provides a medium-term picture of where the school is headed, a high-level road map for the next three years.

We appreciate how difficult this is without medium-term allocations, but not making any attempt to forecast your funding and spending could land you in significant difficulties. It just needs a set of reasonable assumptions.

Without a road map, you may not be aware of how your finances can be affected by a rise or drop in rolls, changes in your per pupil funding as a result of the National Funding Formula, or variations in pupil characteristics that might affect other funding sources like Pupil Premium.

Changes in funding are not the only events that can cause a budget problem. Your need to spend may change, even to achieve the same results. There may be cost pressures that are outside of your control, such as increases in employers' national insurance and pension contributions for staff, or exam fees. The changing profile of your pupils may mean there are more pupils with language delay, SEND, challenging behaviour or other characteristics that affect their ability to learn.

The school's funding may not be sensitive enough to these changes, by which we mean the amount of money you are given might not be enough to keep pace with the increased need to spend. Equally, another source of income might dry up, for example if a community organisation stops using your facilities, leaving you with a shortfall in your overall budget.

Having a strategic financial plan will help to identify the implications on the budget of changes to the way the school is run, such as changes to the curriculum, how classes are organised, leadership and management structures and assessment arrangements.

You may be achieving high standards, but they may be based on a house of straw consisting of overly generous staffing ratios, small class sizes and high salaries which are not sustainable in the long term. If the actions you have to take to address your budget difficulties involve shedding staff, it could put those standards at risk. This is not a sustainable way to go on.

A range of issues can lead to a budget spiralling out of control, and before you know it, the school can fall into deficit. We hope we've convinced you that a deficit is the last thing you need.

By keeping on top of your financial strategy and scanning the horizon for events that might impact on the budget, you are more likely to anticipate problems and take action to prevent them or stop them getting worse. It is far better to act early than to have to find savings to address an unexpected deficit, which by its very existence tends to make everyone nervous.

Now let's move on to look in more detail at the first three key elements of strategic financial planning that we listed at the start of this chapter.

Linking the budget with the school development plan

When strategic financial planning is most successful, it is when it is aligned with the core business of school improvement. It is therefore crucial to establish and maintain a link between two of the most important documents in a school: the budget and the School Development Plan (SDP), sometimes referred to as the School Improvement Plan.

The self-evaluation form (SEF) or equivalent is an internal assessment of a school's position, its strengths and its areas for development. The SDP sets out, usually for up three years, how the school will develop in the areas where the SEF indicates improvement is required. It provides clarity in the school's vision and details the strategies which are to be employed to ensure continuous improvement. The actions identified are detailed to the level of what needs to be done, who is responsible for doing it and by when, and who is responsible for monitoring the action to make sure it's completed in time.

By now, most schools are comfortable with school development planning. For school leaders with little experience in this area, it is usually a top priority to develop this skill. If development planning in schools is distributed across all school leaders, i.e. whole school development planning by senior leaders and faculty level development planning by middle leaders, then there are usually many opportunities for school leaders and aspiring leaders to get involved and make a contribution.

In the current climate, schools need to do more than reference educational outcomes in their analysis for the SEF. Value for money also needs to be assessed, comparing the school's performance against levels of funding. This can be done using the DfE's resource management tools on the gov.uk website, including the individual school scorecard, financial benchmarking and other techniques.

The areas that schools most often struggle with when drafting or updating the school development plan are costing the priorities and linking the plan to the budget. Without strategic financial planning, a school risks running into a deficit or not making effective use of public money for the purpose for which it was intended, i.e. to provide education that results in good or outstanding outcomes for children.

The SDP and budget should be intrinsically linked and should work together, each being equally important to the school's overall success. A budget without a school development plan is not focused, and whilst it may be balanced, spending may not result in any desired impact. An SDP without meaningful costings or any budget provision is simply a list of ideas that may or may not be realised, and progress is likely to be hampered by a lack of resources.

It is vital to recognise when future initiatives require investment, and to make sure that decisions on these initiatives are taken with full exploration of all the options, weighing up costs versus likely benefits.

Since the School Financial Value Standard (SFVS) was introduced, most schools now include a 'costing' or 'resources' column in their SDP. The same is true of academies, who are now required to complete the School Resource Management Self-Assessment Tool annually. The checklist includes the question 'Is the financial strategy integrated with the trust's strategy for raising standards and attainment?'.

The quality of the data that goes into the costing section of the SDP varies from school to school. As a minimum, this area will show a description of resources, e.g. to flag that it will need staff time, reprographics, or training. It is good practice to calculate an actual figure and attach it to the action in the SDP. Often these calculations will be best estimates based on known information at that time, and may need to be updated regularly.

Even if an estimated monetary figure is shown against each action, this does not guarantee that the SDP and budget are linked. Working out the cost is still meaningless if sufficient resources are not allocated in the budget to cover it. A useful way to show the link between the two is to reference the area of the budget to which the action relates.

The LA schools' CFR (Consistent Financial Reporting) format and academy Annual Accounts Return frameworks provide a convenient set of headings for presenting budgets to the Governing Body and LA, but other approaches can also be taken to define the budget heading where resources are allocated. The following table shows how this could be presented for three actions. The status row at the bottom indicates whether the action has not yet been started (red), is underway (amber) or has been achieved (green). Your SDP may have a different presentation format to this.

	Key staff to undertake a curriculum review	Appointment of an additional teacher in Maths	Building project to expand curriculum accommodation
Date	By April 2021	By Sept 2021	Start Jan 2020 End Sept 2020
Personnel	(Name)	(Name)	(Name)
Resource/cost/ CFR code	Staff time £5,000 E01	Staff advertising £950 E08 Leadership time £1,000 E01 Teacher cost £27,000 E01 Staff training £1,000 E09	Capital costs £40,000 C02 Leadership time £5,000 E01/E05
Monitoring	DHT Curriculum	HT and Chair of Governors	School Budget Leader and HT
Status	Red	Amber	Amber

Ideally the resources part of the SDP would be completed by the same person who is setting the budget, usually the School Business Leader (SBL). Other staff may need to advise on what resources are required, in order for the SBL to make a meaningful estimate.

As part of the planning exercise, the lead person needs to ensure that sufficient funds are allocated in the budget to cover the anticipated actions. Sometimes this may mean finding savings in other budget headings to release money for these priorities. If this is not possible, the SDP will need to be refined to show actions which are affordable. This does not necessarily mean omitting an action entirely. Often there are creative alternatives that cost less and can lead to the same desired impact.

It is vital to carry out a strategic overview of the whole SDP and budget, to check that priorities are being reflected correctly in both documents and that resources are being allocated accordingly. A 'first come, first served' approach will not get you very far.

LA schools may find it challenging to link these two documents because the financial year differs from the academic year. The SDP is always written for the academic year.

The key to the two documents being linked in a meaningful way for any school, regardless of their financial year-end, is to have an annual cycle for school improvement planning that incorporates and links all key planning tasks and is shared and understood by all staff. In the last section of chapter 5, we set out the budget cycle alongside the school planning cycle for both LA maintained schools and academies. Achieving this synergy between both cycles will make sure resources are set aside for your key priorities.

As the cycle shows, budget planning should start early, allowing sufficient time for planning the use of resources even before the final funding allocations are known.

When resources are scarce, it's even more important to target them to priorities. You will do this by producing multi-year budget plans with a focus on making sure that you are spending money on the activities that have the greatest impact.

Multi-year budget planning

A multi-year budget plan ensures that sufficient resources are available for every aspect of running the school. It balances forecasts of future funding with known changes in expenditure, taking into account any planned changes in the curriculum, pay profile of staff, anticipated pupil numbers, or any organisational aspects of the way the school is run. Anything that might affect either the funding received or the need to spend must be brought into the multi-year plan.

Of course, the missing element of information in this equation is the amount of funding you are likely to receive over the multi-year period. This is one of the main problems with the current Spending Review system.

In our book **Forecasting Mainstream School Funding**, we provide an end-to-end process with worked examples, showing you how to develop funding forecasts based on best, middle and worst case scenarios for per-pupil funding and rolls. It guides you in preparing your own model so that you can create three possible funding options to test out in your budget plans.

This approach highlights to your staff and governors the uncertainty you are dealing with, taking some of the pressure off you. It can feel as if you are expected to be accurate about future funding, but that simply isn't possible.

We suggest that to be prudent, the worst case scenario can be based on the Minimum Funding Guarantee (MFG) defined in regulations each year. Under the Soft NFF, local authorities are permitted to vary the level of protection, but in 2020/21 and 2021/22 they must award an increase of at least 0.5% per pupil and at most the NFF MFG (1.84% and 2% respectively). Whether they will be able to afford to do this depends on the local context. You can test out different options in your middle and worst-case scenarios.

Scenario planning allows you to estimate how your per-pupil funding might change over the next three years across three options, using the DfE's projections for the pure NFF for your school and local knowledge about your LA's intentions. You will then multiply each of these options by your best, middle and worst-case pupil number forecasts, resulting in nine possible options. From these, you can choose three final scenarios and add estimates of other funding, e.g. Pupil Premium, SEND funding, nursery or post 16 funding. Then you can start to produce multi-year budgets, outlining how you would spend the available funding in each scenario.

As long as you state your assumptions and the reasons for them, the methodology will provide a reasonable high-level set of scenarios to prompt debate and enable you to form a broad plan of action for each situation. Your work can be used as the basis of a Financial Sustainability Plan suitable for high level discussions with governors and senior leaders.

Some budget planning software packages include a less detailed approach to forecasting future funding, or you can devise your own method if you wish. The important thing is to produce scenarios to show different funding levels based on a clear set of assumptions, and get the discussion going. Senior leaders and governors need to be prepared for the possibility that funding may not keep pace with costs, and they need to know how they would respond to such a challenge in future years. Putting your head in the sand really won't help.

Don't forget to make sure that your data returns are accurate, in order to be certain that you are receiving the funding you are entitled to. We mentioned this when discussing how to use information as a basis for budget setting in Chapter 8.

The key to successful multi-year planning is horizon-scanning: being aware of developments that might impact on your funding or spending. Early awareness of changes gives you time to consider what they might mean in your particular context. You can then ensure that you take account of any initiatives needed to address particular areas of teaching and learning, in order to secure the necessary improvement for your local context.

The chapters on annual budgeting in this book discuss obvious areas that can change in the medium term, across pay, non-pay or income. It's a matter of taking a helicopter view and identifying broad-brush answers.

One of the key determinants of your funding is the number of pupils in your school. But it also has a big influence on your spending too. We will now take a look at some of the issues to consider when projecting rolls as a basis for your multi-year strategic financial planning.

Projecting future rolls

It's important to understand the impact of changes in pupil numbers in the medium term, as well as for the annual budget.

Here are some questions that you need to consider in order to compile projections of pupil numbers and identify how they affect your costs. This is all invaluable information to support your medium term financial plan.

- What trends can you spot in pupil numbers over the last few years?
- Do these relate particularly to changes in admissions at the normal points, and what are the reasons?
- Are there plans for housebuilding in the area? If so, it is advisable to contact the local authority for information on planning approvals, the likelihood of families being attracted to the developments, and the timescale for building. They should know if purchasers are likely

to come from within the local area, or whether there is inward movement from elsewhere.

- How would class organisation be affected if pupil numbers changed significantly? At what point will you need to create extra classes, impacting on the number of classroom staff and resources?
- Has there been a decision to save money or restructure staff by increasing class sizes?
- Have new decisions been taken to create extra small groups for pupils with SEND or other additional needs?
- Is the school expanding as a deliberate strategy to address budget difficulties, or in response to local demand? Whichever it is, you need to understand the time lag in funding for extra pupils, which can cost a school a significant amount if growth is rapid. See our reference to Growth Funds in Chapter 6 if the LA asks you to provide new places.
- Have you had building work to enlarge the premises, and do you know how this will affect your running costs?

Intelligence on pupil numbers

The best starting point for information on patterns of pupil numbers is the officer responsible for Place Planning and/or School Organisation in your local authority. The LA has to undertake strategic place planning to meet its statutory duty to secure sufficient places across all schools and academies in the local area. This sort of information is relatively simple to compile at area-wide level, but harder for LAs to predict at individual school level.

Therefore you also need to use your local knowledge of families to estimate the likely new intake, identifying whether cohorts roll forward intact, or whether there is high pupil turnover or an unusual pattern in some year groups. If there is a three-tier system in an adjacent area, you may lose some pupils at transition points to middle or high schools.

Your funding and need to spend can also be affected by changes in the number of pupils with SEND, both in terms of the nature of their needs and in the support required. You need to know how much the support will cost. Similar questions should be asked in relation to support for low attainment linked with deprivation, English as an Additional Language, Looked After Children, those who move school frequently, and those who are persistent absentees. You may be able to identify others.

The most important thing is that you are aware of potential changes and the impact they will have on your funding and need to spend.

18 FACING THE FUTURE

Financial awareness

This book came about because in our work with schools and local authorities over many years, we have realised that many aspiring school leaders receive little training and experience in the financial responsibilities of headship. The School Business Manager role has evolved into the School Business Leader over time, and is now more likely to be involved in strategic financial leadership. Governors are expected to challenge school leaders much more on financial matters.

Where can these key people go for information? There are various sources but they are fragmented.

We therefore decided to write a series of guides to help anyone in these roles, or in any other role supporting schools, to understand the different aspects of school finance and funding. We hope to raise awareness of the key responsibilities, providing frameworks, tools and tips to help you navigate your way through today's challenges of financial health and sustainability.

Ultimately, we want school leaders to be better prepared when they take up their role or move to a new school, so they are able to quickly assess the strengths and areas for improvement in relation to finances. In the current climate, you can't afford to wait.

Key messages

This book focuses on budgeting as an essential task, one that has to be done on an annual basis to comply with the legal requirements of school finances. It can't be put off. You have to achieve a balanced budget each year that satisfies your funding body, working within the limitations of the money you've been given and the set up that already exists, unless you are creating a brand-new school.

We began the book by discussing the challenges facing schools, particularly in the context of the uncertainty over the National Funding Formula, which we've explained in an early chapter. The various iterations of this reform have not changed the fundamental principle: there will be a redistribution of funding over time, although the final decisions brought better protection than was first proposed.

However, the prognosis for schools receiving the minimum increase is that funding is extremely unlikely to cover cost increases over the longer term. It is difficult to assess the true impact on individual schools, firstly because each is at a different starting point in the funding they receive now compared to the NFF, and secondly because other parts of the funding system are still underfunded, particularly SEND. This means that until the Hard NFF is implemented, local authorities may take different decisions to manage the distribution of the funding between schools.

The shortfall in funding and increased expectations on schools to cover missing services in other parts of the public sector have led to a depletion of reserves at an alarming rate in some cases, and others are tipping into deficit or increasing an existing deficit. Whatever you think about the DfE's assertion that there is more money in the system than ever before and that schools can make further efficiency savings, it seems unlikely that this rate of overspending will be allowed to continue.

In the face of a threat to school financial sustainability, leaders therefore need to act to squeeze maximum value from the resources at their disposal. We hope we've shown you a way to decide on the most appropriate tactics to achieve this: taking a measured approach to the school budget, engaging with staff and stakeholders, gathering together all the relevant information, taking care to examine every area for opportunities to make savings, and giving a clear signal of how your use of resources needs to change.

Having a clear vision for what you want to achieve will help you to decide what's important, and by deliberately choosing to fund the right strategies, you will be able to target your resources more effectively. It's also important that the budget is dynamic and responsive to changes, supporting any developments necessary for the school's success.

The content we've provided doesn't only focus on the detailed steps. We've proposed a framework for setting a culture of financial leadership and looked at the roles of the headteacher and governors in relation to finance. Once we have taken you through the budget preparation and monitoring processes, we have explained the principles of strategic financial planning, so that you can go on to look at a longer-term approach, making sure the school has a sustainable future.

If you are facing a more serious financial situation, or simply want to get your budget into the best possible shape, our companion volume 'Leading a School Budget Review' looks in more depth at how to lead a fundamental review, focusing on cultural and behavioural aspects as well as providing practical templates for examining all the different areas of your budget.

Securing value for money is an essential part of your role, at a time when resources may not be sufficient to cover costs without changing the way you do things. Even if you are gaining from the school funding reforms, the pressure for continuous improvement means that you will want to be confident that your money is being spent in a way which helps you to achieve better outcomes. There are many sources of advice, including the DfE's own school resource management web resources and the offer of support from the DfE-funded team of School Resource Management Advisers (SRMAs).

We urge you to remember the cultural aspects that we've referred to. The best way of securing a strong future for the school is to give staff confidence in financial management and develop them as future leaders and managers by giving them the chance of hands-on experience in budgeting and financial control. This will strengthen the professionalism in your school and help future generations of children to get the best possible education.

We hope that this book has been useful in helping to provide an overview as well as more detailed guidance, pulling together all the different strands of school budgeting. Your role is to put it into practice.

The coming years may not be easy; they may involve some difficult choices in order to get your school into a sustainable position within the available resources. But at stake is the future of our children and young people. What better motivation can there be for getting it right?

KEEP IN TOUCH

Thank you for reading the book; we hope you found it useful.

Please leave a review

We welcome feedback and would be very grateful if you could spare a moment to leave a review. It will help us to make future editions of our books better for all readers and it will also help other leaders and governors who may be interested in this book.

Please go to the page where you purchased the book and let us know if we've helped you!

Free monthly newsletter

Julie provides a free monthly newsletter with news of government announcements on school finance and funding and significant reports. Go to the homepage at https://schoolfinancialsuccess.com and sign up via the red button to be better informed without spending ages trawling the internet.

Follow School Financial Success

To access further guidance and to share your experiences with other readers who are on that same journey, we invite you to:

- Visit the School Financial Success blog for regular posts on current topics: https://schoolfinancialsuccess.com/blogs-2/
- Visit and Like our Facebook page @SchoolFinancialSuccess
- Follow us on Twitter: @juliecordiner (Julie Cordiner_School Financial Success)

School Financial Success Publications

For a list of current and planned books, please visit our website: https://schoolfinancialsuccess.com/books/

These include:

- **Leading a School Budget Review**

Being given a leading role in undertaking a detailed review of your budget can be daunting. This book provides a wealth of practical advice for those that have been given this responsibility or may be proposing such a review. Our step-by-step process will be invaluable if you are facing a deficit, or need to redesign your budget to reflect significant changes in your school's operation. It is also very useful for schools who might not be facing significant financial issues at the moment, but want to make sure they have embedded a value for money culture to prepare for the uncertainty of future funding and the challenges that this may bring.

The advice in 'Leading a School Budget Review' will be particularly helpful for those who are asked to take the lead role in a review. It gives tips for managing cultural changes. Not everyone might be supportive of what you are trying to do, and it's best to be prepared for this.

- **Forecasting Mainstream School Funding**

An updated version of Forecasting Your School's Funding, reflecting the latest announcements for 2021/22. This book provides a practical guide on producing multi-year funding projections, the missing piece of the multi-year planning jigsaw. It offers a step by step process with worked examples to help you produce best, middle and worst-case funding scenarios at a high level for the next three years along with a Financial Sustainability Plan.

- **Productivity for School Business Professionals**

Are you a school business professional, are you feeling overwhelmed by all the demands that are placed on you? Does it feel as if work is taking over your life, leaving you exhausted?

This book will help you maximise your personal and professional effectiveness through self-care and a strong focus on what matters most. You'll find a host of tips, techniques and practical activities to help you manage your time, beat procrastination and create productive habits. A companion workbook is available.

Invest in yourself and reap the rewards.

ABOUT THE AUTHORS

Julie Cordiner

Education Funding Specialist

I'm a qualified accountant and independent consultant specialising in school funding and education finance, with over 35 years' experience in local authority education work, including 10 years as an Assistant Director. Between 2007 and 2015 I was a member of the DfE's advisory group on school funding. I advise schools and local authorities on school funding and achieving value for money to support better outcomes and enable children and young people to maximise their potential, something I'm passionate about. Everyone deserves the best possible education and we all need to use taxpayers' money wisely, to achieve a fair chance for every single pupil.

Nikola Flint

School Business Leader

With a background in accountancy and nineteen years' experience in the school business management profession, I fulfil a broad, strategic role as Chief Financial Officer in a multi-academy trust, leading on all aspects of school organisation and SMSC. My experience as a Specialist Leader of Education offering school-to-school support has widened my perspective of the challenges faced by schools and the potential solutions to those challenges. I passionately believe that every child has the right to a high-quality education and that we all have a part to play in achieving this ideal.

NOTES

NOTES

Printed in Great Britain
by Amazon

63239835R00088